MW01446178

TOP SECRET TIPS

HOW TO CRUSH FEDERAL RESUMES

The Things That Federal Insiders Don't Want You To Know

That Will Get You Hired

JOSEPH MERCER

Joseph Mercer
www.career-motivation.com

Printed in the United States of America
First Printing 2020
First Edition 2020

ISBN: 978-1-7347225-1-2

10 9 8 7 6 5 4 3 2 1

TOP SECRET TIPS

HOW TO CRUSH FEDERAL RESUMES

THIS BOOK IS DEDICATED TO
THE LATE DR. THOMAS PAGE

My Friend

TABLE OF CONTENTS

ACKNOWLEDGMENTS

Writing my first book has been a challenging yet rewarding experience. It was harder than I imagined, and I had to rely on the help of friends and family more than ever. So, I want to take the time to acknowledge a few people who have to help me carry my rucksack on this important journey to help others arrive at success.

First, I'm eternally grateful for the love and support of my wife Fatima and kids Tea', Malik, and Naoual during the process of writing this book. They have sacrificed time and attention so that I can fulfill a dream and pass knowledge and inspiration to others.

Next, I would like to thank my brother Dustin who has been a constant cheerleader and source of support for me throughout this entire process. Especially during the times when I thought about throwing in the towel and giving up.

I would also like to thank Mr. George Cushman for his friendship and always being willing to provide a helping hand, objective criticism, and support.

Finally, this project could not have been completed without the advice and guidance of my good friend and mentor, Mr. N.H. "Rush" Rushdan. He has inspired me and taught me to seek "greatness" in my professional life and to seek "goodness" in my personal life.

I hope you enjoy the book and don't forget to do great things!

INTRODUCTION

Welcome!

I would like to congratulate you on taking this important step towards securing a more productive future and lasting employment as a Federal employee. For you to achieve your set goals, you need to acquire knowledge on the subject, and that knowledge paves the way for the actions required to reach your objective of Federal employment. These actions—call them steps—should be specific and accurate to achieve the desired results. In this book, you will learn everything you need to know to move confidently towards your goal of getting that dream Federal position.

The Federal application process is a complex and very convoluted one that requires knowledge and skill to maneuver. For many years, only a few insiders knew and understood the process and how to get hired into the

Federal system. Today, with the implementation of USAJOBS.gov, the process has become more transparent, and more people can understand it and apply for Federal positions. However, one aspect of the process still remains somewhat of an enigma – the Federal resume.

Frequently, the United States Federal Government keeps hiring thousands of people to fill the numerous vacant positions, while many out of the employable population yearn for these Federal jobs; only a handful know what it takes to get these jobs. People desire to work for the federal government for different reasons, but the most obvious of them is job security and massive benefits that accompany these jobs. Even when tons of people keep applying for these jobs, less than a quarter of the number of resumes submitted make it to the final stages of the hiring process. But a larger number of the total submitted applications will not be referred for an interview because of an error on their own part, most likely an improper or a poorly crafted resume.

Having a good resume can be likened to creating a work of art; it requires precision, attention, and expertise, and a liberal dressing of professionalism. Take this, for instance, if there was a need to have a bust sculpture of George Washington or Abraham Lincoln created for the exterior of the White House, the offer might be made public, and a good number of experienced sculptors would likely bid for the contract. But before a particular sculptor is offered the job, the lot would pass through a rigorous process of assessment and selection. And when this is done, the successful sculptor would be adjudged the best among all bidders.

This is the same as the Federal job process. For you to compete in the Federal job market, you must present your skills, knowledge, and abilities in a manner that is easily conveyed to the Human Resource (HR) Specialist and the hiring manager. Thousands of resumes are submitted for Federal job announcement openings, and the average resume may only be considered for a few seconds before a decision is made to either advance or eliminate it from the hiring process. Many well-qualified individuals are often not selected during the screening process because of poorly written resumes. The reason for this, among other things, could be attributed to the emphasis on keywords, which we will address in detail later in this book.

For now, what you need to know is that the HR Specialist sorts resumes by keywords, and keywords determine whether a resume will move to the next stage or not. Keywords give a resume the quality it requires to land you the job of your dreams, and when it concerns Federal jobs, creating a standard resume should be your concern. The reason being that most hiring processes include both: the automated application review process (Applicant Tracking System - ATS) and a manual review process (which involves the HR Specialist). But the thing is that the resumes submitted for application for most Federal jobs are read by real, living HR Specialists. Always have this at the back of your mind when tailoring your resume according to job requirements.

This book has been written to fulfill exactly what its title implies: to learn how to write impactful Federal resumes and stand out from the teeming crowd. This book is a guide. It will help you write an effective resume that is visually appealing, targeted to the job, and will get noticed by employers. The more you know about yourself and the position you are applying for, the easier it will be to create a winning resume.

The purpose of this book is to help you understand the difference between Federal and private jobs and to show you the benefits you stand to enjoy if you choose the former. Good resumes are such a pain to write, aren't they? Well, with this book, you need not worry anymore. What you will learn from this book will make you a pro so much that you will encourage others to get their own copy to learn as you are learning from the book. All you need to do is to pay attention when reading any part you choose according to your current needs.

How to use this book

This book will break down the core aspects of the Federal resume and will equally offer insight into what is required to submit the perfect resume that reflects not only your knowledge, skills, and abilities, but also your experience and qualifications. Top Secret Tips outlines the anatomy of a Federal resume, how to prepare to write a Federal resume, and provides tips and guidelines on writing cover letters. This guide will help you create effective resumes that will get you noticed by HR Specialists and hiring managers.

This book will focus solely on the crafting of your Federal resume. It will not go into job searching, USAJOBS.gov navigation, or the interview process. In these Top Secret Tips, our goal is to conquer the challenges that accompany resume development and inform you of the important aspect of the Federal resume document. No fancy jargon or long stories will be employed – just the down and dirty facts you need to learn how to develop outstanding resume products.

This book covers topics like these and discusses them in plain English:

- Building blocks of a Federal resume
- Conducting a career inventory
- Steps in resume development
- Content required in your resume
- Resume formatting criteria
- Showcasing your expertise
- Correctly writing duty descriptions
- Developing resume headlines

A look at the core aspects of this book tells you that this is not a one-off use. The book is designed to be a guide. Even when you land that particular Federal job you have been gunning for, chances are that one day you may discover you have out-grown the particular demands of the job; hence you would want something more engaging, enterprising, and fulfilling.

The desire of most career people is to have a job that drives them to be better. What most jobs provide for people is the much-celebrated means of livelihood, but these jobs hardly double as the motivating factor most people need to become better at what they do. The lack of enthusiasm among workers is the major reason there is a thing called "the 9-5 slump," but with a good job and an improving career, the rest of the world becomes your oyster.

Therefore, you are expected to use this book as a guide in getting the kind of Federal job you desire and keep it as a reference point for subsequent jobs and career improvement. This goes to say that there is nothing to memorize; just use this book as a reference tool while building your resume, and you will be on your way. This book allows you to go straight to the sections that you need and get the specific information you are looking for to make your resume a work of art.

HOW THE BOOK IS ORGANIZED

This is a reference book, and the intention should not be to read it from cover to cover like a romance novel. Feel free to skim around to find the information you need to tackle the challenge you are facing in your resume development at any particular time. Not everyone will have the same level of experience in writing Federal resumes: some of you are new to the game while others have a great deal of history in Federal resume development. This book is designed to help resume writers at all levels.

When reading this book, ensure you pay attention to the examples and the "Top Secret Tips" that are incorporated into each section. These will provide additional insight into the text and serve as a guide when you write your own resume.

Here is an example of a Top Secret Tip!

Top Secret Tip #1: The more you know about yourself and the position you are applying for, the more successful you will be at crushing the Federal resume creation process.

This tells you that resumes should not be generic. Refrain from using the same resume for different job applications. The first tip that guides you through creating a superb resume is to understand the demands of the job for which you are applying. Understanding the job description and how to create your resume around it will be discussed extensively later.

The information in this book is optimized for quick referencing. This book contains nine parts, and each part is divided into chapters. Each chapter is divided into short sections to help you find relevant information just a little easier.

Although each part furthers the information in the preceding parts, you don't need to read the preceding parts before you understand what any part is talking about.

Here a brief description of the nine parts.

Part 1: The Federal Resume Introduction

This provides an overview of the Federal resume. The section informs the reader (you) of the various reasons people pursue Federal employment, and what a Federal resume really is and how it differs from a traditional resume you submit for employment with a civilian organization.

Part 2: Things You Should Know

There are certain things that you must know about before you begin writing your resume. This section goes over some of the basic concepts affecting the resume-building process that everyone needs to have an understanding of before diving into their resume build.

Part 3: Getting Started

Every project has a starting point, and this section outlines how to get started and the information required to get started on the right track. This part of the book provides you with your collection and action plan to get started creating your masterpiece. You will discover how to capture all the important details about your resume and steps to develop your document.

Part 4: Traps to Avoid

Many highly qualified people do not get selected for a position that they are perfect for simply because they do not know some very simple resume traps. This section of the book reviews those traps and provides insight on how you can avoid having them in your resume submission.

Part 5: Ten Signs of a Great Resume

Want a great resume? Well, this section outlines ten of the signs of greatness in Federal resumes. Most Federal resumes are scrutinized based on ten important factors. In this section, I will review these factors and provide concise information on how you can make sure your resume shows all the signs of greatness.

Part 6: Writing the Perfect Cover Letter

The cover letter is often overlooked and is not considered an integral part of a formal resume. This is a big mistake. The cover letter provides the hiring officials loads of information about you and provides you another opportunity to highlight your skills and express what you can bring to the organization. This section will go over what you need to produce the right cover letter for every job announcement.

Part 7: Proofreading Tips

The proofreading phase of the resume writing process is one of the most critical aspects of resume composition. You can have an outstanding resume that highlights your experience and credentials, but if it's covered with grammatical and formatting errors, these will be a big turnoff to the hiring officials and Human Resources reviewers and provide them with a negative impression of you. This section will explain ways to identify these mistakes and avoid your resume by taking a trip to the recycling bin.

Part 8: Frequently Asked Questions

After years of consulting and writing resumes for clients, there are always some questions that routinely arise. This section will address some of the common questions that applicants have, and that you may have questions about, too.

PART 1: THE FEDERAL RESUME INTRODUCTION

A Federal resume is a document written specifically to apply for a position with the Federal government. This resume is longer than a typical business resume, usually three to five pages in length. In a Federal resume, the applicant attempts to prove to an HR Specialist that you have the required knowledge, skills, and abilities needed for the preferred position. The Federal resume requires a written description of each specialized skill you have developed throughout your career.

A Federal resume is the primary part of the official application for job announcements posted by Federal agencies and organizations. These types of resumes have more specific requirements than those found in the private sector. The Federal resume is not like private-sector resumes, which are formulated for the sole purpose of getting you an interview. The purpose of a Federal resume is to serve as an official document that announces your qualifications to the Federal HR Specialist and the hiring authority. How your resume looks and feels will have a profound impact on the impression you make on a potential employer.

A well-crafted resume can set you apart from other job applicants and deliver pertinent information concerning your experience level and demonstrated knowledge. A strong Federal resume will do more than summarize your educational and employment background; it will emphasize the results of your efforts and draw a concise parallel between your knowledge, skills and abilities, and the employer's needs. Therefore, it is paramount that you keep your Federal resume well-organized and accomplishment-focused.

WHY DO PEOPLE SEEK FEDERAL EMPLOYMENT?

Before we move into the deeper parts of the book, you need to be familiar with the reasons people prefer Federal employment. For most Federal employees, their career is much more than a job. The Federal government impacts the lives of all Americans and military service members. Most Federal employees take pride in using their skills to protect national security, the environment, national airways, fight crime, and help young people receive a quality education.

Some people attribute satisfaction on the job that comes with working Federal jobs as their reason for preferring them to private-sector jobs, and while this might be true, it is also true that benefits and job security are among the top five reasons. Federal government employees enjoy massive benefits, ranging from health insurance, vacation, sick leave, and other income security benefits that are attached to the jobs, which their counterparts in the private sector don't always get to enjoy. Don't forget the reality of job security.

The understanding people have about Federal jobs is that they are more stable than private-sector jobs. If one gets employed in the Federal civil service, they hardly leave the job; all that's required of them is to improve themselves for subsequent promotions. That is why a new Federal employee does their best to ensure they scale through the probation period because they know that their job is guaranteed after that — unless they get involved in corrupt activities or make a costly mistake in the discharge of their duty. Thus, to ensure you get it right from the start, you need to pay deep attention to the rest of the book.

Another reason people seek Federal employment is that the government is always hiring and will be hiring even more government workers to support

Federal agencies over the next few years. Also, job security and other numerous benefits are some of the reasons people prefer Federal jobs. The fact is that the average salary for Federal government jobs competes with the higher paycheck of private and nonprofit sectors.

Well, these are not all. The following are also reasons people prefer Federal jobs:

- They hunger for a chance to be the difference their world needs. This is because Federal government employees are committed to improving the lifestyle of others all over the world.
- Federal jobs are usually location-flexible. For people who want to see the rest of the world, some Federal jobs allow them to work outside of the United States. This is because about 85% of Federal jobs are outside of the Washington DC area, and about 50,000 of the Federal government employees work outside the US.
- Federal jobs offer multiple interests, and this is because there is always a reward for passion for every Federal employment. Whatever skills anyone has, there is an available job offering to match their interest. A lover of animals has a place, likewise a tech guru. There is an array of job diversity, unlike the private or nonprofit sectors. Federal jobs are always challenging and engaging. The jobs also give room for professional growth and career advancement.

These are a few reasons people prefer Federal jobs, and if these reasons are also part of yours, you should take the bold step towards scoring one for yourself. The success of getting a Federal job begins when you can differentiate between Federal and private sector resumes.

FEDERAL VS. PRIVATE SECTOR RESUME

Chances are you have heard about Federal resumes and that they differ dramatically from the typical business resume. This assumption is correct; however, the intent of the resume is still the same – getting you an interview with the hiring manager. The difference lies in the process and the level of detail required in each of the resumes. For example, a private sector HR Specialist does not want details concerning your responsibilities and experience. A Federal HR Specialist does. They want to know the number of people you supervised, what their duties were, and the scope of the work that they performed. This information provides the Federal HR Specialist with the required information needed to assess your level of responsibility, which is then evaluated against the level of responsibility and experience required to qualify for the position.

These differences are very important to you as a potential Federal job applicant. Ignoring these differences could lead to your Federal application being rejected even if you are very qualified for the position. The Federal HR Specialist evaluates your knowledge, skills, and abilities against what is required by the position, and this is a very important part of the hiring process. The evaluation requirement is also the reason why you cannot use one resume for both types of applications. Now let's look into the specific areas where Federal and traditional resumes differ.

You might be wondering why you receive rejection emails when you submit your resume and cover letter to the hiring manager after you have received or read a job alert. The reason is not farfetched – you didn't include enough information, or you didn't follow the right format for writing Federal resumes. As a novice to the process of creating Federal resumes or as a professional, one thing should be at the center of your thoughts: the fact that your resume is the only language that communicates your qualification for a particular position, and if you mess around with this crucial knowledge, you might just see yourself receiving a rejection email like this:

"We have received your application, but deeply regret to announce that you wouldn't be considered at this moment for the job. This decision is based on the demands of the hiring process. Your resume failed to detail the duration and number of hours you spent at the job. Although it documented the number of people you coached, the information was weak. It failed to elaborate on how you lead the team as the leader and how you were able to build a personal relationship with them. Your resume did highlight your core achievements, but it failed to elaborate on their significance to the organization. Please, you might need to pay more attention to the "How to Apply" of subsequent job announcements so that you will be fully aware of what's required for the job."

To get started, you need first to understand that Federal resumes are not written as the private industry resumes, and if you write them like one, you will receive an email like the one above. A Federal resume is first and foremost very competitive; therefore, you are required to put in your best if you want to be successful. What I intend to do with the rest of this chapter is to provide you with an overview of the differences between Federal and private sector resumes, and by doing that, you will get to understand where people win and fail in their pursuit of Federal employment.

At this point, it is taken for granted that you know what a Federal resume actually is, and that it differs from a conventional resume. If you are looking to work in one of the Silicon Valley tech companies, you would be advised to avoid verbosity in your resume. Your career coach will tell you that simple, brief, and concise does it, but it is not the same with Federal resumes. Did you see how the anonymous fellow lost an opportunity to get invited for an interview from the example given above? That tells you that these resumes aren't the same, and as such, there should not be a mix-up in formatting and content when creating them.

> *Top Secret Tip #2: View the Federal resume as a tool that you use in the initial phases of the job application process. Its purpose is to showcase the fact that you have the qualifications for the job you are seeking.*

The private sector resume is often 1-2 pages, and if the applicant's experience isn't much, they are advised to keep it simple and catchy within a page so that the hiring manager will look at it. But, unlike private-sector resumes, where the focus is on highlighting your key achievements, the Federal resume emphasizes detail. Thus, the right number of pages for a Federal resume is between 2-5 pages. And before you go right ahead to create your resume, you should pay attention to these three things: duties and qualifications, how to apply, and how you will be evaluated. Most Federal job announcements include these three things, which are often categorized as the level of experience, education, and training. Thus, you should ensure you have the following: the exact quality of experience required, the educational qualification suitable for the job, and the awards, fellowships, and additional qualifications that boost your eligibility for the position.

The following are some of the key things that differentiate a Federal resume from a civilian resume:

1. **Format:** The formats for Federal resumes are always specific, depending on the job announcement and the body or sector involved in the hiring process. For jobs within the competitive service, applicants are expected to adhere to application instructions issued by the Office of Personnel Management (OPM). The difference in format does not infer that some information should be omitted; rather, it stipulates how the information should be presented. The format often includes specific information, character count, page length, and compulsory field requirements. Some agencies prefer to have their approved templates online and expect applicants to fill them out, while some would want you to upload your resume. In some cases, having to fill out resumes online can be challenging and time-consuming, but it pays in the long run if you adhere to the instructions.

2. **Additional information:** The Federal government often demands the inclusion of specific information in their resumes. This information includes details about your previous jobs (start and end month and year), the address of past employers, previous salary information, college GPA scores, and a whole lot of other information. But the difference is that the information in the Federal resume should be more elaborate.

3. **Required length:** This is another factor that differentiates the Federal resume from the private sector resume. Whereas the length of the private sector resume is between 1-2 pages, the Federal resume is often between 2-5 pages of well-detailed information, with emphasis on a detailed description of your accomplishments. The Federal resume is longer because the Federal HR Specialist needs to see a description of your knowledge, skills, and abilities in

your cited duties and accomplishments. These HR Specialists are looking for qualified applicants; that's why they spend time reviewing resumes to figure out if an applicant has the desired qualifications, skills, and education. In contrast, private HR Specialists do not have time for long resume formats; they want to see bullets highlighting your roles and accomplishments for each job.

4. *Additional requirements:* Apart from the usual job experience that is often attached to resumes, Federal resumes often demand additional details. The additional information makes your resume swim separately in a sea of other resumes. Additional information might come as questionnaires applicants are required to download, fill out and attach to their resume, or they may be required to incorporate the details of the information as a fresh or additional column on their resume.

5. **Details**: As stated previously, a private industry resume typically consists of bullet statements outlining the type of work performed for each position of your employment history. A Federal resume uses sentences to describe major skillsets used during each position and the impact you made on the organization through the implementation of your skill.

6. **Style**: In a private sector resume, the objective is to communicate as much information as quickly as possible. The resume document needs to be eye-catching and easy to scan. This is the reason that bullet points are the preferred launcher to convey information in private industry resumes. Whereas in the Federal resume, you are expected to present the information with as much detail as possible. Rather than bullets, short sentences are used to explain each position in greater detail.

7. **Keywords**: One of the biggest differences between private industry and Federal resumes is the use of keywords. Private resumes do not feature keywords or blend keywords into each bulleted statement. Keywords are VERY important in Federal resumes. Since the Federal HR Specialist receives so many resumes, keywords are placed at the beginning of each paragraph to indicate to the HR specialist what qualifying knowledge, skill, or ability requirement the paragraph addresses.

The above information gives you the basics of writing a Federal resume and shows you how it differs from the private sector resume. We will go deeper into the format requirements of a Federal resume later in this book.

PART 2: THINGS YOU NEED TO KNOW

The focus of this book is strictly on the resume and the resume creation process; however, there are some basic factors that you absolutely need to know to successfully create a Federal resume that will get referred for an interview. These factors are important because they outline the specific information you need to understand about the job announcement to assess whether you qualify for the position. It also includes the specific details you should address in your resume to support qualifying knowledge, skills, and abilities.

Federal job announcements are lengthy and include valuable information about the position, the qualifying requirements, and how to apply for the job. Thus, you must pay close attention to the details of the Federal job announcement.

READING A FEDERAL JOB ANNOUNCEMENT

When you read a job announcement, you should pay close attention to the eligibility of prospective applicants: what's expected of the applicants, the dos and don'ts of the application process, and much more. To elaborate on the last point, when a Federal job announcement seems overwhelming, this is when some applicants make mistakes, and when these mistakes go against the instructions of the job announcement, the result is a non-referral.

Pay close attention to the following sections of the job announcement:

- Job title, job series, and job grade. You want to make sure that these are in line with your career experience and your desired career field.
- Check the closing date to ensure you have time to prepare your resume and application for submission.
- Check "Who may be considered." You want to make sure you are eligible for the position and will be considered for hiring actions.
- Read the qualification factors to ensure you meet them. This section outlines the qualifications an applicant should possess. If you fancy a particular position, but you lack the qualification needed for it, the best thing to do is to apply for the position you are qualified for, and then work towards gaining the qualification for the position you desire. Once you get a Federal job, it is easier to transfer than to get in from the outside.

- Identify the type of application and submission process (i.e., hard copy for mail or fax, or text file for the USAJOBS resume builder or other federal agency site builder).

- Review the "Required Documents" section. When you get here, read carefully to understand what documents are required for submission and the order they should be submitted in. The required documents often include your Federal resume, scanned copies of your certifications, and your cover letter. Cover letters are not always demanded, however.

- How to Apply: This section is very vital. This is where the dos and don'ts are spelled out. Therefore, you should pay close attention to it. In fact, all sections of the application process are important. When you read this section, make sure you understand every aspect of it clearly. Have it in mind that you don't have the liberty to guess because doing so might negatively affect your application along the way.

Top Secret Tip #3: Make sure to read each Federal job announcement entirely and thoroughly. When you do, you will see a few job descriptions that fit your career avenue and your specific qualifications.

When you make your pick of position, read the job description entirely. Understanding the demands of the job will help you create a compelling resume. As you read the announcement, pull keywords from the text sections for your resume. The job announcement is divided into the following seven sections:

- Overview: The overview section provides a summary of all the essential details concerning the job announcement and the position. This section provides the opening and closing dates; it contains the salary range/scheme; it also has the schedule for working (the number of hours and days), and it also includes the pay scale of employees according to their grade.

- Location: This concerns the number of available vacant positions that will be filled and their locations. Knowing the location right from the outset helps in decision-making. The location section also gives more detail on the position. Some Federal government jobs have flexible locations. Some of them are stationed in telework centers, and the location explains whether the position is available for this workstyle or not.

- Duties: This elaborates on the demands of the job.

- Requirements: In this section, you will see how you will be assessed. The requirements section outlines the kind of skills and experience required for the position. It also spells out the requirements for the background investigation level and the ratings. How you will be rated is based on how you filled out the application questionnaire, which is often located in the "How You Will Be Evaluated" section. Reviewing this questionnaire is another way you can develop a list of your core abilities for the position. You should know that you can review these questions before proceeding with your application. Before submitting your application, carefully go through the questionnaire and confirm that everything stated in your resume tallies with the information you are providing.

- Required Documents: This includes all the certifications you have, which are required to prove your eligibility for the position. These documents are often required before the application process can be completed.

- Benefits: This section addresses one of the reasons people prefer Federal employment. It tells you about other compensation plans that come with the position.
- How to Apply: This is the guide to applying for the job. It gives you instructions on how to apply. It also gives you the window of feedback (when you should expect to hear from the hiring agency). This section also gives you further tips and material needed for a smooth application, such as the benefit of starting early, encouraging you to follow instructions, explaining the application process, and exposing you to the details you should pay closer attention to. It closes by reminding you to save a copy of your application for reference purposes.

MINIMUM QUALIFICATIONS

The term "Minimum Qualifications" is a very important one in Federal job announcements, so much so that I decided to devote a section to explaining this term and making sure you understand its meaning and how it applies to your Federal job application.

Minimum qualifications are standards set by the U.S. Office of Personnel Management (OPM) to help ensure that Federal employees are indeed qualified for employment. You must meet these minimum qualifications to be considered for employment. Minimum qualifications are stated in terms of general or specialized experience. Specialized experience is usually obtained from having worked in a position similar to the job being filled.

For some jobs, you can qualify based solely on education instead of experience. For other jobs, both education and experience are required. And for yet other jobs, you can qualify based on a combination of your experience and education. These requirements will be described in the vacancy announcement.

The important thing to remember about these minimum qualifications is that if you do not prove to the Federal HR Specialist that you meet them, your application will not be considered. So read the minimum qualifications carefully and make sure to tailor your resume and state facts to show that you meet these qualifications.

TIME-IN-GRADE

Time-in-grade is a requirement that applies to the promotion of current and former Federal employees. Generally, employees must serve one year at the next lower grade level. Time-in-grade restrictions do not apply to former Federal employees who have had a break in service of more than one year, current Federal employees on temporary appointments, or current Federal employees not holding a General Schedule (GS) position. Time-in-grade also does not apply to applicants who have no Federal work experience.

> *Top Secret Tip #4: Make sure to thoroughly review the requirements in the vacancy announcement to include the minimum requirements and time-in-grade. Doing so will ensure that your resume has all the necessary information in it to meet these standards.*

PART 3: GETTING STARTED

Every resume project has a starting point, and this section outlines how to get started and the information required to get started on the right track. This part of the book provides you with a collection of action plans to start creating your masterpiece. You will discover how to capture all the important details about your resume and the steps to develop your document.

For starters, you need to understand that the Federal resume is your smart key to gaining entrance into the Federal employment service, and for that entrance to be smooth, you must take into strict consideration the process it must pass through to match the job announcement. To get this right, you should do two things: study the job announcement thoroughly and assemble the right tools that will help you build a superb resume. This includes making inquiries about the government parastatal you are applying to. You can see this information in the "About Us" page on the official website of the agency.

Often official websites will require you to create a profile before you can have access to the organization's public information; you should do this. Knowing how the agency operates is a huge plus when applying for a job. Sometimes data you pull from the "About Us" page goes a long way in directing you on how to tailor your resume and how to craft your cover letter to express your abilities and accomplishments. There are some resumes and cover letters that just speak to HR Specialists. We want yours to be one of those.

Your resume should follow the USAJOBS.gov format. One trick is to use an online resume builder or download and use one of the several Federal resume templates available online to build your resume and download it on your profile afterward. Using this trick will not provide you with a finished product in most cases, but it will ensure that you have all the relevant information on your resume.

Again, once you read a job announcement thoroughly, the first smart move should be to visit the "About Us" page of the organization. On there, you are likely to pull keywords that will resonate with the job announcement. When you have done this, compare the keywords you have pulled with the keywords from the job announcement and tailor your resume around them. If, for instance, the job announcement says that you would attend to actual and virtual complaints and refer the problem to the appropriate resource center or agency when necessary, you should understand that it involves receiving and, maybe, returning phone calls. So, you should let your resume resonate keywords like this:

Receptionist – Data and Information Center 2011-07 – 2015-07

FOX Technology Solutions, Miami, FL

Salary: $20,587 Hours/Week: 40

GS-0503-1

Supervisor: Arianna Hughes, 796-708-2440, may contact

Top Secret Tip #5: Make sure your resume has all the necessary information concerning your employment history listed. This includes past supervisor and salary information; not doing so could result in your resume not being processed for the position.

Duties:

- Received and returned 200+ phone calls every day.
- Maintained courteous and professional relationships with customers, clients, and callers.
- Advised clients and callers accordingly and transferred their calls to appropriate staff members when needed.
- Took and relayed phone messages to appropriate resource personnel.
- Forwarded calls to voicemail when appropriate.
- Referred misdirected calls to the proper personnel, resource center, or agency.
- Answered low-level questions without consulting superiors.
- Received in-person visitors and responded to their inquiries to save time for senior staff.

- Responded to voicemail messages via phone and answered simple email inquiries when appropriate.

Key Accomplishments:

1. Took part in rewriting the automated phone menu, which resulted in about 45% reduction in office calls, thereby routing most calls to the organization's website.

2. Saved up to 30% staff time more than the previous information and data center receptionist by learning the answers to most frequent questions and inquiries without having to consult superiors and also by having a catalog of new products, service offerings, and resources ready in a happenstance of inquiry.

When you read a job announcement such as the one mentioned above, to put your best foot forward, you need to understand what the job requires from you. And to make the HR Specialist move your resume to the interview stage, you have to let them see how equal to the task you are. But if the job announcement is for entry-level candidates, you should foreground your educational achievements. Let the HR Specialist see these in light of professional achievements.

If you were a captain of your school's football team, state it on your resume and state what you achieved while you occupied that position. If you were a cheerleader, also state it and state the accomplishments that came with it. If you participated in other school activities such as volunteering for community work or you introduced a new and continuous activity into the school's extracurricular activities, by all means, state it. You may not have the professional experience, but being active and resourceful speaks volumes of what you could achieve when given the opportunity. You should have something like this when your academic achievements announce your resume:

Barry University, Miami, FL   October 10, 1998 – July 15, 2002.

Graduated 07/2002.

Excelled in swimming classes.

Led class and school volleyball teams as captain.

Participated in cheerleading from sophomore to senior year.

Suggested and participated in creating a class volunteer group named "Get it Right." The group developed into the school charity group. Yearbook "Get it Right" pioneer leaders column can attest to this.

Graduated with GPA: 3.9 out of 4.0.

So, the things you must know before you delve into resume writing have been captured above, but for the sake of emphasis they will be summarized in the following bullets:

- You should clarify your promise of value.
- You should ensure your target is adequately defined.
- Your resume should scream the result.
- You should not underestimate the effectiveness of keywords.

These points are your sure way to get started, and when you source for information and build your resume around them, you will definitely crush Federal resumes. More information on these points will be shown later in the book.

FEDERAL RESUME ANATOMY

Now it's time to get started with your Federal resume. The resume development can be a daunting task, but in this book, we're going to show you how to address your resume build step-by-step.

Heading

This section of a resume is one of the most important. It should include your name, address, email address, and phone number. Make sure to let your name STAND OUT by using bold and enlarging the font size of your name. You should use a professional email address. One of the most important sections of your Federal resume is the heading. This section should always be placed at the very top of the resume page. The header section contains the applicant's name, address, email address, and telephone number. Make sure to use your formal name and avoid using any abbreviation, and always use a professional email address in the header section.

Your name should be at the top center of the page in bold print and a slightly larger font than the other text in your resume. You may wish to include both your school address (in the upper left) and permanent address (upper right). Use headings to organize your resume. Headings should reflect the information that the reader will find in that section. Take a look at the example below.

JOHN DOE
Teesdale Road, Lockridge, AL 09114 •Cell 000-000-0000 •DSN 314-123-1234
•Email: johndoe@gmail.com
•Veteran Preference: 30 Points •Top Security Clearance

Summary of Qualifications

The Summary of Qualifications is not a required section of the federal resume. However, it can be a plus, if used effectively, to highlight the specific qualifications of the position and your level of experience in those qualifying areas. This section highlights your key selling points. It is an overview of the relatable experience you have accumulated throughout your career. I typically use three to five bullet statements, depending on the number of qualifying requirements in the job announcement, to highlight the number of years of experience in a specific area.

Keep in mind, these are short statements about your specific qualifications, career goals, or employment objective. They can help the HR Specialist understand your career needs by letting them know what type of work you are looking for. If an average employer is only going to spend 20 seconds looking at your resume, it's important to be clear about your goal. There are a few things you should know about this section:

- This statement is optional but can be a valuable addition to your resume.

- If you are doing a targeted resume, you may want to include an objective. If you are completing a master resume, you likely won't include one.

- If you are applying for a specific job (e.g., advertised or through a contact), you may not need an objective as the reader knows what you are applying for. Instead, you may find it helpful, to begin with, a strong career highlights section to create a positive first impression. This section should provide an employer with a picture of your most important and relevant skills and qualifications.

- Highlight key qualifications that make you a good candidate for the position.

- It usually includes three-to-five key points that you want an employer to know. Remember, a master resume will include all highlight statements regardless of the job you are applying for.
- Keep in mind that the "Highlights of Qualifications" section will appear before the skills section on a resume. However, you may find it is easier to summarize your qualifications once you've developed your skills section. Most current Federal resumes include either a bulleted or paragraph summary of the candidate's key selling points. It is accomplishment-oriented and includes many keywords in the target job category. Feel free to use either the bullet or paragraph format, but never combine the two. A typical group of highlights includes:
  o How much relevant experience you have in the targeted field.
  o What your formal training and credentials are, if relevant.
  o One significant accomplishment, very broadly stated.
  o One or two outstanding skills or abilities relevant to the field.
  o A reference to your values, commitment, or philosophy, if appropriate.

Top Secret Tip #6: Always center your summary of qualifications statements around accomplishments that focus on the qualification requirements listed in the job announcement. You want to tell the reader upfront that your resume will prove that you qualify for the position.

The Summary of Qualifications section is a great place to highlight where you meet or exceed the minimum requirements for the position. If the position requires at least one year's experience making balloons, this is where you can say:

- Ten years of proven experience in balloon production

Education

This section of a resume lists all the colleges you have graduated from, along with their addresses. It also lists the degrees you have earned with the dates you attained them. If you are in the process of attaining a degree, list the expected date that you will receive it. Do not list your high school unless it is recommended.

You should list institution name, post-secondary degree(s) received, and dates earned or expected (place in reverse chronological order). Include major/minor areas of concentration, specialization, or certifications. List city and state when looking outside of the state, where employers may be unfamiliar with the location of your college. Don't include institutions you attended but from which you failed to graduate with a degree. Entry-level applicants without relevant job experience but with the required job qualification should include their GPA in their resume, especially those with a very high GPA (4.0 and above).

Include relevant courses and skills/knowledge gained and also include special projects. You can equally include honors, awards, scholarships, theses, research projects, percent of college expenses earned, and any beneficial extracurricular activity you took an active part in. (This category may come in a separate section or divided into subsections, depending on the information presented.)

Most recent college graduates put their education before their experience because it is often more relevant to their objective. But if it isn't, put your experience first. List the degree you are pursuing or have earned, the institution you are attending with the city and state, and your graduation date. You can also include any academic honors you have. It is also a good idea to list relevant courses if you have no experience in the field. This will help employers ascertain your knowledge in the field. You may also want to describe any research or design projects you participated in. The education section is usually of particular importance to university students with limited work experience and for others who want to highlight their degree(s).

Experience

The experience section is the most important one of your resume. This is where you should focus your energy on captivating the review panel. This section should display your skills and achievements in line with what they are looking for. Ensure you describe your work experiences as achievements and not just assigned roles.

The experience section of a resume can refer to paid or unpaid jobs and should include your job title, the name of your employer (that's the organization), the city and state in which the company is domiciled, and the dates of employment (that's the start and end dates). When you have listed these things, you are expected to summarize your contributions to the organization via the position you occupied. Give numbers when applicable. Make sure to use action verbs to begin your statements. Use a present verb tense only when describing a current position. This should not be a job description but instead should be an avenue to illustrate your accomplishments and results.

Top Secret Tip #7: Use numbers, statistics, and quantifiable data when describing your achievements. This gives the HR Specialist a means to equate these to the position in which you are applying.

You can draw from a variety of areas to develop this section. Besides traditional employment, you can include relevant experience gained through temporary jobs, work-study, internships, volunteering, military experience, significant academic assignments, or extracurricular activities. Each entry should state the name of the employer or organization, the location, dates of employment or involvement, the position, and a brief description of your responsibilities and accomplishments. If your experience is not directly relevant to the field to which you are applying, emphasize those duties or responsibilities that demonstrate transferable skills such as leadership, initiative, teamwork, adherence to deadlines, creativity, or special knowledge and specific skills (e.g., technical writing/research, statistical analysis, public relations, project management, or any other skill).

Your experience, regardless of how you acquired it (full time or part-time jobs, internships, and community or college service) is usually of chief interest to the HR Specialist. When describing your previous roles, begin each sentence with a keyword header. Keyword headers like supervised, controlled, organized, managed, and directed transmit responsibility, and the recruiting panel needs to see that.

Since Federal resumes follow chronological formats, you should begin with your current or most recent position and work backward. Include part-time work and unpaid work, such as internships and volunteerism.

Honors and Awards

This is an optional section of your resume that could come in handy. It is important to list any relevant awards. The preferred format is: the award received, the issuing body, the year received, and the location received. These can be school or non-school-related. Make sure to include the date you received the honor or award. For clarification, it may be necessary to give short descriptions of the nature or purpose of some of the organizations, awards, honor societies, or service organizations. Only include scholarships that are based on merit, not financial need.

When listing your honors and awards, highlight achievements such as scholarships, Dean's List, leadership roles in clubs, campus/community organizations, sports, or other accomplishments. Include these in the most appropriate section of your resume. For instance, include academic awards in the Education section, include work-related accomplishments in the Employment section, and include volunteer achievements or sports awards in the Volunteer Activities/Community Involvement section.

Skills/Highlights

In this section, you should inform the reader of any unique, relevant, or necessary skills that you have but are not reflected in the other sections of your resume. For example, foreign language skills. You should indicate whether it's conversational, fluent, or bilingual. You should also include the technical skills you have in computer applications. You can also outline the skills or abilities you learned from activities such as team sports, volunteering, and hobbies. There are a few things you should put into consideration when writing your skills/highlight section:

- Avoid including information about religious or political affiliations unless they are important to the job (that's if you are applying to work for a political or religious organization).

- Avoid listing hobbies that a reader might be uncomfortable about (for instance, target shooting), but for targeted resumes, you can list these if they're relevant to the position you're applying for.
- Avoid adding obsolete or irrelevant experience. For instance, experience from ten or more years ago. You should focus on including experience that is relevant to the position you're applying for.
- You can also include activities that support your objective. Be sure to think about why you are including each piece of information and remember that it is better to highlight a major accomplishment. For instance, "Had a story published in the Fall of the previous year." This is reasonable and clear enough, compared to simply providing a list of everything you have ever done.

Volunteer Activities/Community Involvement

This section is optional. You should title this category or categories according to the type of information you are presenting. The activities can include professional/student associations and positions held, athletic participation, extracurricular activities, special skills (computer, languages, etc.), certifications, licensures, publications, military or community service experience, interests, and a host of other extracurricular activities.

References

This section should be on a separate sheet of paper that matches the font and format of your resume and cover letter. The heading on this page should also match your resume. You should always secure the permission of anyone you choose to use as a reference before giving their name.

Good references might include professors, advisors, or previous employers. Never use relatives as references. Give a copy of your resume to these references so they can speak highly of you when your potential employers talk with them. Employers might ask your reference questions like: "How reliable is this individual?" "What was it like to work with this individual?" and "What kind of contributions did this individual make in the organization through their job?" Be sure to list your references in order of how well they know your qualifications and include their name, title, company, city, state, zip, phone, and email address, where applicable and when appropriate.

It is not necessary to include the statement "references available upon request" on your resume. You should prepare a separate document to list your references using the same heading and paper as your resume. Include a brief statement of how you know them. Generally, employers will request that you provide them with three to five references that they may contact. Before selecting references for an employer, you should:

- Identify three to four references who will comment fairly and positively and can speak clearly about your strengths and contributions.
- Ask for permission to use them as a reference.
- Include the reference's full name.
- Include their current job title and name of the employer.
- Specify their relationship to you (supervisor, co-worker, client).
- Ask for their preferred contact information (that is: office, home, cell phone number, and/or email address). Also, ask them for the best time and means to contact them.

CAREER INVENTORY

The Career Inventory is a series of forms and worksheets that I have developed that will assist you in gathering all the necessary information you need to build your resume. Consider these products as your road map and reference points as you go through the resume development process.

Resume Checklist

You should go through your resume to ensure that everything checks out. Your checklist should present the details in your resume accordingly. This means you have gone through it to determine that the following are in order:

- Employer names, addresses, and telephone numbers and dates of employment.
- Former supervisor's names and telephone numbers (you should provide at least three professional references, using past and current supervisors if possible).
- Your job title.
- List of your responsibilities.
- Salary/GS level and step.
- Training.
- Career accomplishments.
- Awards received.
- Education.

This does not mean that these sections should follow this order. All you need to do is set your own order and tick them off when you are satisfied with what you have written.

Check out the **Resume Check List** below for more information.

Overview	Yes	No
Is the resume the appropriate length for the experience level and grade (2-5 pages)?		
Is the layout of the resume inviting, with consistent formatting, fonts, and font sizes?		
All information is presented in a logical and well organized manner.		
Are all the sections of the resume clearly label?		
All margins are consistent and even on all sides.		

Heading	Yes	No
Does heading include your name, address, email address, and phone number?		
Are you using your formal name without abbreviations?		
Is you email address professional?		

Education	Yes	No
Does the education section outline your school name and address?		
Is the major and minor indicated for all degree plans?		
Does the section highlight training, certifications and licenses relevant to the position?		
Does the section list the institution with the city and state, and your graduation date?		
Education information includes academic honors received.		

Experience	Yes	No
Is experience listed in reverse chronological order (present or newest job first)?		
Does each position include a solid listing of accomplishments?		
Does the section present experience using the CAR format?		
Does each description statement begin with a strong action verb?		
Does the experience being highlighted seem relevant to the requirements of the position?		
Are specific keywords from the job announcement and other sources being used?		
Is required information (company address, supervisor's name, etc.) included?		

Honors and Awards	Yes	No
Only scholarships that are based on merit, not financial need are included.		
Descriptions are included with each award to highlight the nature of the accomplishment.		
Military awards are listed in chronological order with a brief description on the award.		

Proofreading	Yes	No
Spell check is used to identify commonly misspelled words.		
A manual proofreading was conducted to check for wrong word forms ("form" and "from").		
Read resume section by section and compare format and arrangement of each section.		
Has a second person read over your resume paying attention to style an grammar?		
Have you avoided the use of personal pronouns (I, me, and my)?		
The resume is error-free (no spelling errors, typos, grammar mistakes, etc.).		
The formatting is consistent (bold, underlining, and fonts).		

Go to www.career-motivation.com to download a free copy of this worksheet.

Experience Worksheet

This is a worksheet that studies your work experience and accomplishments on a deeper level. It helps you identify an experience or accomplishment you might have missed. As you complete the activity, do the following:

- Give yourself a job title whenever possible.

- List everything, even if it doesn't seem important to you.

- Include any equipment you operated or software you used.

- Think about transferable skills that can be applied in different settings. For instance, how you coached a soccer team, or your communication, financial, and leadership skills. Let's say you were the treasurer of your horseback riding club; it means you probably have some basic bookkeeping skills.

- Record your accomplishments. An instance can be cited from when you received positive feedback, praise, or were recognized with a formal award for what you had done.

Having an experience worksheet helps you remember and include all your relevant accomplishments.

Check out the **Experience Worksheet** below for more information.

Company Name				
City			State	
State Date		End Date		

Position Title	
Duty Description	

List below where you made an impact on this organization	
1	
2	
3	
4	

What actions did you take to achieve the impacts listed above? (write them in CAR story format): Challenge / Action / Result. Include tangible (quantitative and qualitative) descriptions for these impacts.
CAR #1
Challenge Statement
Action Statement
Result Statement
CAR #2
Challenge Statement
Action Statement
Result Statement
CAR #3
Challenge Statement
Action Statement
Result Statement
CAR #4
Challenge Statement
Action Statement
Result Statement

Go to www.career-motivation.com to download a free copy of this worksheet.

Accomplishments Worksheet

In the Accomplishments Worksheet, you will create an inventory of your accomplishments — tasks you enjoyed doing, did well, and are proud of. Include education/training, volunteer experience, jobs, projects, travel, group or team activities, and skills. There is no one formula for what to include in a resume. Your resume should uniquely reflect you! Focus on the outcomes of your efforts, including the skills you have developed. Quantify your results if possible. Don't sell yourself short! Resumes are promotional tools.

Check out the **Accomplishments Worksheet** below for more information.

Professional:

Accomplishment	Skills

Personal / Social / Civic:

Accomplishment	Skills

Go to www.career-motivation.com to download a free copy of this worksheet.

RESUME DEVELOPMENT PROCESS

This section will review the resume development process and how all the worksheets and lists you just completed fit together to create magic. To understand the resume development process, you first have to understand its intent. The intent of the process is to break the resume creation kaiso down into four distinct parts – I call them phases.

The four phases of the resume development process are collect, prepare, create, and review. Each one of these phases builds upon each other to create a finished resume product. Let's now dissect this process so that you can have a better understanding.

Check out the **Development Process** below for more information.

COLLECT	**Collection Checklist**
	☐ Keywords from job announcement
	☐ Old resumes (if applicable)
	☐ Employment information
	☐ College Transcripts
	☐ Contact information for current and past supervisors
	☐ Addresses for current and past employers
	☐ Addresses for volunteer and civic organization
	☐ Copies of awards and recognitions (if applicable)

PREPARE	**Experience Worksheet**	**Accomplishments Worksheet**	**Education Worksheet**
	• Enter experience info for each position	• Enter professional & personal/social/civic accomplishments	• Enter info for each advanced education
	• Provide short duty description for positions	• Provide relevant skills associated with each accomplishment	• Provide short description of relevant studies
	• List organizational impacts		• List awards & honors
	• Enter C.A.R statements		• Provide overall GPA

CREATE	**Format Checklist**	**Resume Creation**
	☐ Select resume format	• Apply selected format from Format Checklist
	☐ Define resume sections	• Import header from Format Checklist
	☐ Select font & points size	• Import work history from Experience Worksheet
	☐ Determine overall resume look/design	• Import accomplishments from Accomplishments Worksheet
	☐ Develop Resume Header	• Import education history from Education Worksheet
		• Import awards and recognitions from Collection Checklist

REVIEW	**Resume Checklist**	**Proofreading**	**Trusted Reviewer**
	• Check overall format	☐ Identify misspelled words	• Evaluate attractiveness
	• Check Heading section	☐ Wrong word forms	• Check for grammar mistakes
	• Check Education section	☐ Format inconsistencies	• Evaluates style and grammar
	• Check Experience section	☐ Grammar mistakes	• Examines the overall resume look/design
	• Check Honors & Awards section	☐ No Personal pronouns	
		☐ No weak action verbs	

Go to www.career-motivation.com to download a free copy of this worksheet.

The Collect Phase

In this phase, we gather all the necessary information and documentation required to construct our resume. This includes the job announcement (with keywords indicated); any old resumes you may have on hand; employment information (salaries, awards, etc.); college and trade school transcripts; contact information for past supervisors; physical addresses for current and previous employers; addresses and contact information for volunteer and civic organizations; and copies of any awards or recognitions you may have received.

The Prepare Phase

In the preparation phase, you will use the information you gathered previously in the collect phase and turning it into manageable information utilizing the experience, accomplishments, and education worksheets. Take your time during this phase, and make sure you annotate all your experience, accomplishments, and education. Next, review this information with the job announcement and eliminate all the irrelevant references on these documents. Finally, consider your keywords from the job announcement and see if there are opportunities where you can rephrase some of your statements using the type of language used in the job announcement.

> *Top Secret Tip #8: Don't forget (and this is a big one), your resume must cover all of the topics on the occupational assessment questionnaire. You can view this questionnaire by clicking the "view the Occupational Questionnaire" link under the "How to Apply" section of the job announcement.*

The Create Phase

Now its time to get started on the actual resume product. By now, you should have all the information you need to build a fantastic resume product. But before we can begin inputting the information, you have to consider how your resume needs to be formatted.

> *Top Secret Tip #9: Carefully consider which sections you include in your resume and how they are arranged. You want to make sure that the factors that qualify you for the position are highlighted prominently and upfront.*

Selecting your format might sound trivial, but it is actually one of the most critical steps in resume creation. This is because you need to develop a format the complements the things that qualify you for the position. For instance, if your qualifying factor for the job is education and training, you would not want a format that highlighted your work experience by having it at the top of the resume. In contrast, if the announcement states that only experience will be considered a qualifying factor, you would not want to overly address your educational background.

After the format checklist is completed, you will begin drafting your resume. At this point, all the hard decisions and composing should have been completed. All you should have to do is apply your format and import the information from the worksheets. But don't relax too much, because the process is not finished yet. Now comes yet another critical step – the review.

The Review Phase

The review phase is the most critical because it polishes your resume and makes it shine. You can do a fantastic job outlining your knowledge, skills, and abilities, but if your resume is littered with grammatical errors and formatting mistakes, it will only detract from your message. That is why the review phase is broken down into three simple steps: the resume checklist review, the proofreading review, and the trusted reviewer evaluation.

In the resume checklist review, you will be conducting a macro evaluation of your resume. In this review, you will be addressing the overall format and its consistency, the layout to include margins and spacing, the titling and heading formats, and the overall appearance. You want to make sure that your resume looks professional and inviting.

Top Secret Tip #10: Take a break between the creation and review phases. You will come back to the project with a fresh perspective, and you are likely to see more issues.

In the proofreading review, you will be conducting a thorough micro evaluation of the document. During this pass, you will address issues such as misspelled words, wrong word forms, formatting inconsistencies, grammar mistakes, the use of personal pronouns, and the use of weak action verbs. We'll go into proofreading and action verbs in more detail later in this book. Once you have proofread your resume a minimum of three times, then it is time for the next step – the trusted reviewer.

The trusted reviewer is someone that can objectively and critically review your resume and provide you with feedback on its attractiveness, grammar, style, and overall design. The trusted reviewer should be someone familiar with Federal resumes and their design. It's essential to get an objective opinion on your resume before you submit it to ensure that you are relating your information clearly and concisely. Also, be sure to provide the trusted reviewer with a copy of the job announcement so that he or she can use it to give context to the information you are providing.

And just like that, the resume process is complete, and you are on your way to gaining Federal employment. Remember, the best resumes are customized for a specific job. However, there are common elements that appear in nearly all resumes, regardless of the type. With one particular position in mind, use the activities mentioned throughout this book to start developing your resume. Keep in mind what style of resume you want to use. There are the chronological, functional, and combination resume formats — but for Federal resumes, stick with the chronological format.

Analyze the Job Announcement

The content of the job announcement should be your blueprint. All information and ideas you need to base your resume on should come from the job announcement. Therefore, you should pay close attention to every part of it.

Identify Relevant Skills

Highlight your experience, so that it focuses on skills and achievements that are desirable for a particular position. Make sure each accomplishment listed outlines a skill the employer is seeking, often listed in the position responsibilities and qualifications.

Remember, transferable skills are skills you've developed that can be used in many different settings. If you are applying to your first position in a particular field, consider in detail which skills you have developed from past experiences that may translate to this new environment.

Write Descriptive Phrases

This is a practical aspect of your resume. When writing to them, you should focus on:

- Using action verbs: This means writing concise phrases to describe experiences that demonstrate your relevant skills. The accomplishments on your resume should ultimately be targeted to address an employer's needs. Do your best to place them in order of relevance with the most relevant information as close as possible to the top.
- Within four pages, aim to develop a focused, succinct marketing document that clearly communicates your value and relevant experience and skills.
- When describing your experience, use detailed descriptions that give the HR Specialist a picture of you as an individual (e.g., "Adapted lesson on dinosaurs to learning styles of autistic children"). This is more descriptive instead of making vague statements or descriptions that make you sound like everyone else (e.g., "Followed the curriculum of cooperating teacher").

- You should describe each position, stressing the major accomplishments and responsibilities that demonstrate your competency. Don't include all responsibilities; some are assumed by employers. Start each phrase with an action word. Tailor your descriptions to your job target. Do not repeat skills that are common to several positions.

Choose a Format

Your resume should not be longer than four pages. In certain circumstances, it can be five, but typically for a college student, it could be two pages. Do not justify the pages. Allow the right border to run wild. Font point could be between 10–12, excluding the point used in writing your name.

REQUIRED FEDERAL RESUME CONTENT

While format, length, information, and additional requirements of creating Federal resumes have been mentioned, there are other equally important things you must know before you begin to write it. They are the sort of things that will make your resume stand out. This section goes over some of the basic concepts affecting the resume-building process that most people overlook, yet need to have an understanding of before diving in.

Regardless of all the points that have been mentioned, experience in the relevant field ranks the highest. After all, employers are looking for people who will contribute to the growth of their organizations. Hence, you should boost your resume with experience. You need not land the job before you have experience in relevant fields; if your dream is to get a job within the excepted services, you can build your experience cache by volunteering for civilian employment. You can become a civilian consultant with the Police department or any other role of the sort. This way, you get hands-on experience even before you start working for the Federal government.

You should also know how to make your resume scream your experience right in the faces of the HR Specialist. When you write your experience, never forget to include things such as the duration of time you worked on the job, the hours you expended on it, the experience you gathered while working on it, and how what you did contribute to the advancement of the organization (always emphasize this part).

Your experience/accomplishments section should downplay your financial gain while working on the job but should foreground the organizational benefits. Organizational benefits are what the hiring manager is looking out for in your resume, and you will let them see them by doing the following:

- Let the hiring manager know the level of experience you gathered while you were a team leader, a project manager, or just a team member. Mind you, you do not need to occupy a leadership position for your impact to be felt; rather, it should be seen in what you achieved irrespective of the position you held. Let's look at this for instance: there's a job placement within the Government and Public Services, the career level if, for experienced personnel, the successful candidate is required to work full-time, and the job function is "Management: Program Manager." If you see a Federal job alert of this sort, what you are required to do is to go right ahead and read the job summary, read up its key responsibilities and requirements (which include conditions of employment such as qualifications, specialized experience, education and other things the hiring agency might decide to add). When you have digested the information correctly, you stand a better chance of coming up with a better resume, tailored to the demands of the job.

- The stellar resume you create will include experience in volunteer work and roles in the community or government organizations, and how you accomplished a whole lot for the organization or community during your time there (mind you, this is for people who do not have professional experience in relevant field, let's say a fresh college graduate). It should also include your experience on the job (that's the main job). For a just-out-of-college candidate, the roles should capture the semblance of things you would equally achieve with an official appointment. The HR Specialist needs to know that you take your job seriously and that you are results-oriented, regardless of financial benefits or position. Read on to see how to go about capturing it on your resume.

> *Top Secret Tip #11: It is important to be descriptive and thorough when telling about your skills and experience. Consider HR Specialist and the hiring authority as being unfamiliar with tasks, systems, acronyms, terms, and other information pertaining to your current and past employment.*

There should be detailed examples of how you saved money for the organization or community, how you earned money for them, how you managed the little funds and resources you were given and were able to achieve maximum benefits despite obvious financial and human resources constraints, or it could be an example of how you achieved all three. You could list them in the following way:

- Completed daily, weekly, and monthly reports earlier and more accurately than the former inventory manager.
- Organized a charity event that generated 70% of the funds for the Peacock Foundation, Inc., Dade County, Miami, Florida.
- Supervised a team of millennials that worked an extra ten hours a week for four months to raise 40% of the amount of money that was invested in the subsidiary of the company.

There is one important thing I want you to note about the accomplishments above, and that is the use of keywords. Look at the words "completed," "organized," and "supervised." These are keywords that speak volumes of your achievements in relation to the positions you occupied. References on the importance of keywords will be made continuously in the book. Furthermore, you should notice how the organizational benefit was detailed in the accomplishments.

1. You should also know that you are required to customize your resume. Most times, when people are advised to customize their resumes, they mistake it for personality. You are not encouraged to make the resume all about you; your resume should be all about the job you are applying for. You should tailor your resume to suit the current job announcement rather than using your generic private sector resume to apply for a Federal job. When you customize your resume according to job announcement at hand, you get to announce the following to the HR Specialist:

   a. Your competencies
   b. Your skills
   c. Your knowledge
   d. Your experience
   e. Your qualifications.

   When you announce the following to the HR Specialist, you are indirectly showing them why they should hire you. And you are indirectly telling them that not doing just that would be their loss. Customizing your resume emphasizes your abilities to the hiring manager, and the best way to achieve this to leave out irrelevant experience when tailoring your resume. It also includes importing the terms in the job announcement into your resume. If in the requirements the announcement states that candidates must be conversant with Google tools such as Google spreadsheets, Hangouts, and the rest of them, you should mention these tools in your resume. You don't just mention them, you elaborate on how you used them to meet organizational needs.

2. Your resume should be professional, simple, and written in chronological order. There is a lot to be discussed under the organization, and this will be handled as the book progresses. In

all, the idea is to be tidy and not to confuse the HR Specialist with scattered information or obsolete words.

3. You should be concise in your resume. Yes, you have been encouraged to be detailed, especially in your accomplishments section, but you should not allow this to make your resume too wordy. HR Specialists receive tons of resumes for a particular position. Thus, your ability to be detailed yet using as few and relevant words as possible will be your leverage over other resumes.

4. Review your resume for grammatical errors and other inconsistencies that might impede your chances of being successful.

Contact Information

Your contact information should contain your full name, your mailing address with zip code, area code and phone number, your email address, country of citizenship, and your eligibility for veteran's preference. Veteran's preference refers to employment regulations that prevent veterans seeking Federal employment from being penalized for their time in military service. There are mistakes you should avoid making when you write your contact information. You should always be professional. Don't include inappropriate email addresses. If your current email address isn't professional, create a new one for free online. Follow www.hotmail.com, www.gmail.com, mail.yahoo.com to create a professional email address.

Employment Information

This information should include job title, dates of employment, salary, hours worked per week, employer's name and address, supervisor's name, contact phone number, and whether or not they may be contacted. In your employment information, you are expected to have salary information and employment dates.

Resume Formatting

- ***Length***

  There are multiple formatting options to be considered; pick one of the options and be consistent with it throughout the resume. Your resume should not be longer than four pages. In certain circumstances, it can be five, but typically for a college student, it should fit into two pages.

- ***Fonts and Graphics***

  10.5–12 points, basic typeface such as Arial is preferable. Scanners work best with simplicity, so avoid the use of italics, underlining and fancy fonts, columns, shading, and boxes.

- ***Paper***

  Regular paper is fine for your own copies. In most other cases, you will want to use a quality heavier bond paper. You should be conservative with the color: white, beige, tan, gray, so that an employer may subsequently photocopy or fax it to others involved in the hiring process. Your letters, resume, and references should all be printed on the same paper. The paper should always be 8½ x 11 in size.

- ***Email/Mailing***

  When emailing your resume, make sure that it is sent in PDF format. When mailing your resume, make sure not to staple it, and it should be accompanied by a cover letter.

SHOWCASING YOUR AWESOMENESS

Who Are You?

This presents your details to the HR Specialist.

What Have You Done?

Here you describe each position, stressing the significant accomplishments and responsibilities that demonstrate your competency. Don't include all responsibilities; some are assumed by employers. Start each phrase with an action word. Tailor your descriptions to your job target. Do not repeat skills that are common to several positions.

Where Have You Been?

When writing your bulleted statements for positions held, think of where you added value to an organization and quantify where possible. Did you increase sales? If so, how much did you increase sales? Did you streamline processes? If you trained or supervised, how many individuals did you lead? Stay away from solely listing your job duties. You will want your resume to highlight the skills you have obtained from your various experiences.

Top Secret Tip #12: Use keywords and action words to describe your skills and experiences and always show how you used these attributes to add value to your organization.

How Do You Provide Value?

Use action verbs to describe your duties and accomplishments, depicting yourself as someone who gets the job done: one who "created . . . published . . . solved" – not one who merely "participated in" or was "responsible for." Avoid using "assisted" – say what you did. Vary the vocabulary. For present employment, use present tense verbs and for past jobs, apply past tense.

WRITING DUTY DESCRIPTIONS

1. *Detailed Descriptions*

Emphasize skills and experience related to the job you want and to the employer's needs.

2. *CAR Format*

This format simply stands for Challenge, Action, and Results. It could be expanded on as bullet points. Although taking a glance at it one might mistake it for FAQ, it is a practical explanation for your accomplishments. Resume bullets should describe your skills and achievements, reflecting the order of priority that the employer has stated in their position description and requirements. Write bullet points for jobs, internships, volunteer experiences, and activities where you've developed skills. Consider how these bullet points highlight skills and experiences that match the position requirements. Make action-oriented statements, and when highlighting your accomplishments, you should use concrete language and could include:

- What: What task (transferable skill) did you perform? Use action verbs!
- Why: Why did you perform this task? Was it to fulfill a goal, serve a need, or make your organization/company better?

- How: Specifically, how did you perform this task? What equipment, tool, software program, or method did you use to accomplish it?
- Result: What was the positive result you achieved or the impact you have made by performing this task? Was it quantitative or qualitative?
- Adjectives: Spice it up with descriptors; sell yourself… go for it!

3. *Action verbs*

These verbs are your keywords. They are things to show the relevance of your skill, experience, and accomplishments. They should be powerful enough to respond to the following questions:

- Why is this important?
- What were the results?
- How did it contribute to the growth of the organization?
- How many? How much? How often? So what?
- Did it save time? Money? Did it increase profit?
- Can I quantify this item?
- Have I provided enough specifics?

The action verbs you use on the first page of your resume should be a strong starting point that should attract and sustain the gaze of the HR specialist. Thus, you must put the most related and impressive accomplishments first within each job description. See a list of some action verbs you can use.

RESUME ACTION VERBS

Accomplishments	achieved expanded improved pioneered reduced resolved	restored spearheaded transformed operationalized	Management	administered analyzed assigned attained oversaw consolidated	improved delegated organized developed directed recommended
Communication	wrote collaborated influenced negotiated promoted addressed	arbitrated arranged authored drafted directed convinced	Technical	assembled built calculated computed designed devised	engineered fabricated maintained operated programmed upgraded
Teaching	advised clarified coached instructed coordinated developed	enabled encouraged explained facilitated informed coached	Financial	administered allocated analyzed appraised audited balanced	forecasted managed marketed planned projected researched
Creative	acted fashioned created customized developed directed	initiated instituted integrated introduced invented originated	Helping	assessed assisted clarified coached counseled demonstrated	familiarized guided motivated referred rehabilitated represented
Clerical	approved arranged catalogued classified collected compiled	dispatched executed generated implemented inspected monitored	Detail Oriented	operated organized prepared processed purchased recorded	retrieved screened specified systematized tabulated validated
Data	Calculated Compared Composed Computed Complied Conducted	Planned Recorded Reported Researched Synthesized Theorized	People	Advised Assessed Coordinated Consulted Counseled Entertained	Instructed Interviewed Led Managed Motivated Negotiated

Avoid weak verbs such as: assisted, aided, helped, handled, participated in, responsible for, used, worked with, oversaw, etc. Instead, select verbs that create a picture of you in action. Follow the verb with the success or result of that action.

Referencing

It is no longer necessary to state at the bottom of one's resume that "References are available upon request" since it is understood that employers will ask for references if they are interested in you, whether or not you state this. Instead of having your references at the bottom of your resume, you should have them in a separate document.

Top Secret Tip #13: Always request permission before offering someone as a reference. Also, provide them with a copy of your most current resume.

Phone/Email References

Many employers want to be able to check your references by phone and, increasingly, these days, by email. Ask three or four people who know your work – professors, supervisors, officials, coaches, advisors, etc. Include their full name, their title, organization, address, phone numbers, and email addresses.

Always get permission from these individuals before putting them on the list and prepare them for potential calls from employers. (Send them a thank-you letter for being a reference, update them on how your job search is progressing, and enclose a resume.)

Written References

In addition to asking for permission to list someone as a professional reference, you may ask for a written recommendation letter from the individual. When you are asked for references, you can use the list and/or any letters you believe are relevant. Offer them at an interview, or if references are requested in the job posting, you may attach it with your resume. This is what we mean by references furnished upon request. As mentioned, including this phrase on your resume is not necessary and, since space is at a premium, you can use that space for something much more informative.

PART 4: FEDERAL RESUME TRAPS TO AVOID

A re there really resume traps to avoid? This is a frequently asked question. Many highly qualified people are not selected for a position that they are perfect simply because they do not know some basic resume traps to avoid. These traps are simple mistakes people make when writing their Federal resume. This section of the book reviews those traps and provides insight on how you can avoid them. The following are a few mistakes you shouldn't make when creating your Federal resume:

- Never use the Resu-mix format. This format lumps everything concerning a section in one lengthy paragraph. For instance, when you open the column for Experience, you are expected to fill in all information about experience and accomplishments in one paragraph. If a resume is written like that, the HR Specialist might find it unreadable. Always remember that there could be up to five hundred resumes for the HR Specialist to read. Always make yours scannable so that key achievements will be prominent. To make your resume interesting to read, list your key accomplishments in bullet points or as short precise paragraphs. This way, each paragraph will be written to capture one skill set or accomplishment.

- Never present your accomplishments, weakly. This cannot be emphasized enough. The work experience section is the most essential section of your Federal resume. Therefore, craft resumes, so they do what they are meant to, which is getting you referred for the position. When you present your accomplishments in a sea of words, you leave the HR Specialist confused as to what exactly your accomplishments are. Your accomplishments paragraphs should be well-organized to generate visual traffic to them.

- Never include skills and experience you do not have. A Federal job announcement might demand applicants to take a self-assessment questionnaire online before they could proceed with the application. If you include skills and experiences you do not possess and cannot elaborate on in your resume, you will ruin your chances of getting referred. So, this is what you should do: instead of having the inconsistency in your questionnaire and resume may affect your chances of scoring the job, maybe because you don't have enough experience or skills, you should foreground your academic accomplishments instead.

- Never underestimate what keywords can do to boost your resume. You can boost your resume with keywords by doing all you have been taught so far.

- Never overlook the relevant knowledge, skills, and abilities (KSAs) mentioned in the job announcement. Even when you have top-notch experience and accomplishment in tech design, if the job announcement is for vacancies in administration, your resume might not make it to the interview stage. So, when you update your resume, find a way around the KSAs you are lacking. HR Specialists also look out for these when they go through resumes. You might not have the certification for the KSAs, but you can let the HR Specialist know that you possess the KSAs from the way you write your resume around them. Your job is to tailor your resume to the job posting; cut out the unnecessary details.

Top Secret Tip #14: Address all qualification skills listed in a job announcement. Even if you are weak in a particular area, it is better to cover each qualifying factor than to have your resume dismissed for not meeting all the job qualification requirements.

- Never let the number of pages scare the HR Specialist. The USAJOBS resume builder does not insist on any maximum number of pages, but you should not let this fool you. The fact that you can upload a twenty-page resume on the builder should not tempt you to overwhelm and bore the HR Specialist with words. If you are a professional who has had a stretch of experience, since you are using the chronological order, try striking off the professional skills and accomplishments that do not really highlight your offer of value on the job.

- Never dwell on jobs that have no relevance to the current application. Although you have been told to only include relevant experience in your resume, if you are only just starting to build a career and if the jobs you've worked at have little to do with what you're applying for, mention these experiences en passé but foreground your achievements while at the jobs. The experience might not be needed, but the accomplishments are the selling angle you need.

- Do not make spelling and other grammatical errors. Never omit your email and phone contact information. One significant difference between Federal resumes and private sector resumes is the tone. While private-sector resumes primarily focus on highlighting your skills and accomplishments, Federal resumes are written in an expressive yet formal tone.

- There are a few mistakes to avoid, and although some have been listed in part one, there is every need to elaborate and include more traps you should avoid. These avoidable traps are:

- Avoid making vague statements: Give more than the bare essentials, especially when describing related work experience, skills, accomplishments, activities, and club memberships that will give employers desired information.

- Avoid making typographical, grammatical, and spelling errors: These suggest carelessness.

- Have at least two others proofread your resume before submitting it. Do not rely on spell or grammar checkers on your computer alone.

- Do not make your resume hard to read: A poorly typed or copied resume looks unprofessional. Use a plain font (Times Roman, Helvetica, etc.), and a point size no smaller than a 10 point (11 in the body of your resume). Asterisks, bullets, underlining, bold, and italics should only be used to make the document more comfortable to read.

- It should not be too verbose: Using too many words to say too little. Do not use incomplete sentences or paragraphs. Say as much as possible with as few words as possible (this is where the action words come in handy!). Be careful in your use of jargon and avoid slang.

- Do not make it too sparse: Give more than the bare essentials, especially when describing related work experience, skills, accomplishments, activities, and club memberships that will give employers desired information.

- Do not include irrelevant information: Customize each resume to each position you see (when possible). Of course, include all education and work experience, but emphasize only relevant experience, skills, and accomplishments. Do not include marital status, age, sex, children, height, religious memberships, and other personal details.

- It should not be generic. Tailor your resume according to the job announcement.

- Do not make it too snazzy: Too many resumes scream, "I need a job; any job!" The employer needs to feel that you are interested in the growth you will bring to the company through that position.

- It should not be boring: Avoid flowery or wordy job objectives; stick to the position you are applying for. Also, ensure that your objective focuses on the organization's need, not yours (e.g.: avoid objectives like "To get a good job that pays well and uses my skills").

- It should not be too modest: Of course, use good quality paper, but avoid colored or pre-decorated paper. Become familiar with converting your resume from Word to .pdf files, as companies are requesting resumes via email.

PART 5: TEN SIGNS OF A GREAT RESUME

W ant a great resume? Well, this section outlines ten things to look out for in a great Federal resume. Most Federal resumes are scrutinized based on ten essential factors. In the private sector, the resume's function is to get you an interview; however, the purpose of the Federal resume is to show the HR Specialist your qualifications. In this section, I will review these factors and provide concise information on how you can make sure your resume shows all the signs of greatness by having the following qualities:

1. *Organization:*

The HR Specialist should be arrested by the organization and presentation of your resume. This tells you not to make your resume look sloppy or untidy.

2. *Detail:*

Your resume should be very detailed but less wordy. When your resume is adequately detailed, it should have: the date you started work on each job and the date you stopped, the number of hours you worked for each job experience you list, the level of experience you gained on each job, your accomplishments on the job, and the awards you were given (if any) for your extraordinary exploits.

3. *Personality:*

Although you were told not to make the resume all about you but about the job, you still need to add a touch of worth on the resume, and this will be more strategic in your accomplishments paragraph. When you highlight the skills you learned while volunteering, elaborate on the accomplishments that accompany that experience. When you do this, you make your resume great. Remember, a powerful resume celebrates accomplishments over gain. Such a resume usually gives a promise of value. For instance, you could state your accomplishments this way: "Increased profit by 65% before the end of the second quarter of 2013. The increase generated up to $3 million for the company." "Developed a feasible plan that helped the company maintain 85% of its returning clientele, unlike the turn-up that was witnessed in the previous year." "Got promoted to field manager as a reward for the unrivaled efforts." A great resume should be self-promoting and never include things you didn't do in your Federal resumes. When it comes to referencing, the lie won't hold.

Top Secret Tip #15: When possible end your experience "C.A.R." statements with quantitative and tangible results. Do not be modest, tell the hiring officials what you did that made an impact on the organizations in which you have worked.

---

4. **Social skills:**

   Your resume should show that you have enough social skills to give value to the job. It should also highlight what you were able to achieve as a team leader or member. It should show how you were able to save time and money by being proactive and creative. Your social skills and your ability to manage time should highlight how good you are. This highlights your ability to think out of the box and proffer solutions. You don't get to write these with flowery words, you should show *how* in your accomplishments. These achievements would have more value if you were able to score them with minimal supervision. Social skills are seen in action words like organized, supervised, led, initiated, managed, suggested, anchored, and advised. When presenting your skills, limit the use of words like "assisted" and "contributed." These words do not highlight your strengths. These aren't the only set of words that highlight your ability to be proactive and work under minimal or no supervision, so use them as much as you can.

5. **Sustainable value:**

   Your resume should contain the keywords that HR Specialists are looking for. These keywords should let them see in clear terms what you have achieved and how you are willing to bring a higher level of the same spirit and zest into the job.

6. *Consistency:*

   Your resume should maintain a consistent format. This is seen in terms of font size, style, and sectioning. Consistency shows tidiness and clarity, things HR Specialists are also looking out for.

7. *Practicality:*

   Your resume should highlight your abilities, accomplishments, and skills with clear examples. It's not enough to write "proactive" and "team spirit" in your resume without showing the HR Specialist how you were able to achieve them.

8. *Professionalism:*

   Your resume should be professional and business-like. Refrain from using the first-person pronouns and also understand how to use your action words. You could have, for instance: "Developed software that works as a virtual assistant to members of staff. The software helps them to organize their schedule, manage their time, listen in to meetings when absent, and receive, send and read memos offline." Also, be professional in your resume by avoiding the use of acronyms. If you must include an acronym, also include the full name of the acronym.

9. *Address every period of time and gap:*

   Because your experience section is expected to flow from year to year, you should address any gaps in your work history. Don't just leave them for the HR Specialist to figure out.

10. *Sync skills and achievements in your resume and cover letter:*

    There are skill sets that show the HR Specialist how exceptional you are. Therefore, when you include a generous number of them in your resume and your cover letter, you have the advantage of being referred. Such a skill set includes communication skills, people skills, leadership skills, marketing skills, and time and self-management skills.

These are ten signs of a great Federal resume, and when you write your resume bearing these in mind, you will definitely excel.

More Signs of a Great Federal Resume

Make your resume as dynamic as possible. Begin every statement with an action verb. Use only relatable active verbs that describe what you accomplished on the job. Don't include white lies to please the HR Specialist; you should only write what you did. Take advantage of your rich vocabulary and avoid repeating words, especially the first word in a section. The resume showcases your qualifications in competition with the other applications. Put your best foot forward without misrepresentation, falsification, or arrogance; the reason is that employers want to know what you can do for them. That being said, whenever possible, tailor each resume for the job.

You should not use a to-whom-it-may-concern resume to apply for Federal jobs. While you may qualify for several different positions, it is better to create a different resume for each job and incorporate only the information pertinent to that job description. This will reduce the tendency to crowd your resume with too much non-related information.

Your resume should be well written. This is important when sending a paper version of your resume to employers. The look of your resume should be eye-catching, not distracting. Be consistent with spacing and margins, allow for lots of white space and borders, and emphasize important points with font and text styles that won't distract the HR Specialist.

If you choose to boldface a job title, to be consistent, you must boldface all job titles. Be aware that information presented on the first page, at the beginning of a section, in the left-hand margin, or in a column, gets extra attention. For example, dates in the left-hand margin are emphasized. If your job chronology is not something you want to highlight, place the dates in a less conspicuous place.

Adding descriptive action verbs such as established, implemented, created, and streamlined to your sentences is a huge plus. It is crucial to start each sentence with an action verb. Employers scan resumes and decide in less than 30 seconds if they want to look more closely at what you offer. Edit with care and delete information that isn't relevant.

The first quarter of your resume should dazzle the HR Specialist. The "Job Objective" or "Summary of Qualifications" section powerfully illustrates your top selling points. Laying more emphasis on this section is an ideal way to get noticed fast. Make sure to show your accomplishments, skills, and abilities. Employers want to see proof that you can do the job. Be sure to demonstrate the result of your experience and how others benefited from these results. You can effectively achieve this by including evidence of your productivity, by noting any cost or time savings and mentioning innovations, changes, or actions that show you produced results.

> *Top Secret Tip #16: Be sure to position your most qualifying skill factors in the first top quarter of the front page.*

Remember to list your skills, qualifications, and experiences in as positive a manner as possible, but also remember not to exaggerate or misstate the truth. Be sure your job responsibilities are adequately described by your job title and indicate the actual level of your abilities. Exaggerating your skills will not do you any good!

Including any personal data such as age or height, is seen as unprofessional. Employers must be careful not to violate any discrimination laws, and most organizations prefer that you don't include it. You should avoid including personal information such as:

- A picture
- Your social security number
- Your birth date
- Marital status, height, and weight
- The words "I," "my," or other forms of the first person (e.g., "I was responsible for…") should be omitted
- Always write full sentences or paragraphs
- "Responsibilities included…" Your resume should be more than a listing of tasks. Make it come alive!
- References or a line stating that "references are available upon request" should not be included
- Exclude personal details such as marital status, age, Social Insurance Number, ethnic background, and religious or political affiliation unless it is essential to the job (e.g., applying for a job at a church where you are a member, applying to work for a provincial or federal politician). You should not include: Photographs unless for modeling or acting-related resumes.
- Don't make it too long. Select only the most significant and recent honors/activities to include.

Review your resume and have someone else read your resume as well. This is the most important thing you can do once you have written your resume. Mistakes of any kind are incredibly annoying to HR Specialists, and they are also the fastest way to get your resume into the rejection pile.

Spelling mistakes and typos suggest the poor quality of work they can expect from you. In all, a great Federal resume should be:

- Targeted
- Consistent
- Well-written
- Concise
- Self-promoting
- Accurate
- Abbreviation-free
- Personal information-free
- Grammatically correct

PART 6: WRITING THE PERFECT COVER LETTER

A ttaching a cover letter to your resume is your way of introducing yourself to an organization. One of the mistakes people make is that they send their resume without a cover letter. And just like the resume, your cover letter should not be generic; it should be customized to highlight your interest and commitment to filling the vacant position you are applying for. Your cover letter exists to draw more attention to your resume. Basically, it is assumed to be the first official contact you have with a prospective employer. Your cover letter should have the following qualities to be perfect:

- Purpose
- Organization
- Clarity of expression
- Error-free
- Should fit into a single A4 sized paper.

Top Secret Tip #17: Never submit a Federal resume without a cover letter! The resume justifies that you qualify for the job with knowledge, skills, and abilities. The Cover letter shows that you fit the job in personality and attitude.

Your cover letter should contain the following: how you learned of the job vacancy announcement, why you are interested in the organization, why the organization should hire you, and the time and mode of follow-up. There are a few things you should be familiar with before you start writing your cover letter. They include:

- Thorough research about the vacant position and the organization. You already know where to get this information.
- A draft plan of what you would want to include in your cover letter.
- How to do a comprehensive spell-check before submitting it.
- Contact your references before you include their details.

The above-listed tips are the most important things to bear in mind before writing a cover letter. Your cover letter is not perfect if it does not motivate the HR Specialist to go through your resume. Below is an example of the contents of a cover letter:

You should include your details:

- Your name
- Your residential address
- Your contact (preferably mobile number)
- Your email address

Then you are expected to give a single line space before writing the date. The next section bears the prospective employer's details:

- The company's name.
- The recruiter's name.
- The company's address.
- Phone, Fax, Email (where applicable).
- Salutation (Dear -----------, If you can, you should address the HR by name, but if their name isn't available, you can use the department/agency name for Federal applications)
- Re: the position you're applying for.

Paragraph 1: State your reason for applying for the job. I am applying to indicate my interest in the above position you advertised on USAJOBS on February 14, 2020.

Paragraph 2: This is where you state your interest in the job (Why are you applying for the position? Why you think you have the needed skills and qualifications for the job).

Paragraph 3: This shows why the organization should consider you. This paragraph is expected to be persuasive by referring to the HR Specialist to your resume, where you have provided more details about the sustainable value you are bringing into the organization. In this paragraph, you give the briefest summation of your key achievements and qualifications.

Paragraph 4: This announces how confident you are that you have expressed yourself and that you are waiting for a positive response from them. It is also in this paragraph you close the letter with something like this: Warm Regards, then your name and signature.

A well-written cover letter should always accompany your resume or application. Its purpose is to introduce yourself, expand on the experience in your resume as it relates to the job description, and explain why you are interested in that specific company/organization. A good cover letter should:

- Open with a compelling paragraph that tells a story and catches the reader's attention.
- Connect your experiences and qualifications with the desired requirements of the employer.
- Include specific information about why you want to work for the employer and industry.
- Exemplify clear and concise writing skills with zero grammar/spelling errors.
- Demonstrate your knowledge of the position and of the company.

THE PURPOSE OF A COVER LETTER

A cover letter is really a form of a business letter. Each resume you mail, email or fax must be accompanied by a well-written cover letter. When responding to posted vacancies, each cover letter should:

- Show how your background meets the employer's needs (as stated in their job description), as well as why you want to work for that organization, in that position, or with that situation.
- When sending a resume to an organization for which you have not seen posted vacancies, write a letter of inquiry, in which you ask about current or potential vacancies, state why you are interested,

and what makes you the right candidate. Ensure that your resume gets to the right person in the organization.

- Make clear the position for which you are applying.
- State how you found out about the organization or the vacancy. Mention (If appropriate), the name of the person who suggested you send the resume.
- Emphasize the specific skills you have that are required for this particular job.
- Say why you are interested in this job and/or want to work for this organization.
- Demonstrate your writing abilities, attention to detail, and research.
- Include relevant motivation (why you have chosen this field), attitudes (how you view your long-term goals), or personal traits (your unique qualities), all of which don't belong on a resume.
- Make mention of any future communication.

The purpose of a cover letter is to build a bridge between your resume and the job description. You must help the employer see how your experiences, which are listed on your resume, could help you be successful in the job described. A cover letter should always accompany your resume unless specified in the job posting.

COVER LETTER ANATOMY

Header

You should include a cover letter with every resume or application you send. Your cover letter is really a sales letter that tells the target employer why hiring you would be beneficial for their organization. It calls attention to your resume, in which you outline in detail what you can do for the employer. Go the extra mile to find a specific name to whom you address your letter. As in any business letter, the cover letter contains three main parts:

- The introduction
- The body
- The closing.

You should begin by addressing your reader's needs rather than describing your own. Include your contact information at the top of your cover letter. You may use a standard letter format, or you may use the same header as you do for your resume.

Opening paragraph

Grab the employer's attention. What do you know about the company that makes you want to work there? Identify the position to which you would like to apply and demonstrate your knowledge about the position. You should also identify how you learned about the position opening. You could explain how you learned of the position by mentioning the name of a person who works at the organization or referencing a job posting from a website or newspaper. The introductory paragraph needs to announce the purpose of the letter, which is your intention to apply for a particular job opening that you saw in an ad or heard about, and it should give the reader a compelling reason to read on.

When writing, use a strong opening statement that grabs the reader's attention. If a mutual friend told you about the job, use their name as an introduction as long as you have their permission. Do research on the company and demonstrate your initiative and knowledge by working in fact about the company that isn't common knowledge.

Body

This section will contain one or two paragraphs, in which you describe why you are qualified. Don't repeat the same information from your resume. Instead, use the body of your letter to expand on some of the information from your resume. Include relevant details about specific projects or experiences. You may use paragraph form, bullets, or a combination of the two. It is beneficial to repeat phrases from the job description in the body of your cover letter. This is an excellent strategy for helping employers see that you have what they want.

Does the job description mention that the ideal candidate should have "excellent interpersonal communication skills?" Then your letter should read something like "Among the skills I have to offer are my excellent communication skills. For example…" Immediately back up every statement like this with some solid facts. Talk about something you've done that demonstrates your skills.

The middle paragraph explains why you think you are qualified for the job and, more importantly, what you can offer to the company. Explain your current situation briefly and why the position you are writing about interests you. Expand upon one or two points from your resume. Make reference to the job description and tell the HR Specialist what specific qualities you can bring to the job.

Ask for an interview! Describe what step you will take next, and be sure to follow through with what you say you will do. It is appropriate to say that you will call them on a particular day to follow-up. You may want to include your contact information here and invite them to contact you with any questions for the position.

Closing

The closing paragraph specifies the desired next action. You can tell the reader that you will call, or you can ask them to call you to set up a meeting. Be sure to provide a way for them to reach you easily during business hours. There are a few more details you should pay attention to or include in your cover letter to attract your desired audience, and they include:

- Research the employer's organization to see how your experience, skills, and abilities meet its needs. In your cover letter, show why you are a good fit. Send the letter to a specific person whenever possible; otherwise, use "Dear Hiring Manager," "Dear Members of the Selection Committee," "Dear HR Specialist," or "Dear Hiring Team."

Top Secret Tip #18: Always research the employer before creating your resume and cover letter. You can learn much about an organization's culture and mission from just doing a web search.

- Carefully review the position responsibilities and qualifications and design your cover letter to match these as much as possible. Sometimes position listings are vague. In these cases, draw from your experience of similar positions to infer which skills and abilities might be required or similar research positions online.

- Good cover letters are brief and to the point. (For example, a phrase such as "I would like to take this opportunity to inform you that . . ." does not say anything.)

- Make it clear that the letter is addressed to a specific person at a particular place for a specific job. Do not use generic "one-size-fits-all" ideas such as, "I can make a valuable contribution to your organization." What specific contributions? How are these important to this organization? In your letter, show how your skills match the requirements of the employer, incorporate what you learned from your research, the job description, or an information interview.

- Be sure to say why you want to work for that organization and be sure you say why you feel qualified to perform the functions of that job. Make sure you change any named organization or job title from a previous cover letter.

- You should not put "My name is ___" in your letter.

- Do not start every sentence with the word "I." Instead of "I received my Bachelor of Avionics degree in May. . ." – say, "In May, I received . . ."

- The letter should sound like you, not like you have lifted the verbiage from a cover letter manual. The tone should be professional without seeming overly formal. Imagine what you would say when asked about what you do, rather than what you think "sounds good."

- Relate your specific experience to the job, but do not restate each item from your resume.

- Use industry "jargon" sparingly, especially when changing fields. Many initial screeners won't be able to interpret obscure-sounding statements. Your aim is to get this letter past the initial contact – directly to the person who will be making hiring decisions.

- Read your letter aloud. Does each sentence make sense? Do all the sentences in a paragraph share related ideas? Most paragraphs should be more than one sentence.

- Think about your background in relation to the position responsibilities and qualifications. Ask yourself, "What have I done that is similar to what this position entails?" Consider courses are taken, classroom projects, work experience, summer jobs, internships, volunteer experience, extracurricular involvement, and travel. Be sure to indicate in the first paragraph what position you're seeking. If a specific person recommended you for or alerted you about the position, including their name and title upfront.

- Compose the letter in business letter format: your address, date, their address, colon after the salutation, leave space to sign the letter, type your name under the signature, type the word 'Enclosure' at the bottom if you enclose your resume.

- Preferably address your letter to the hiring manager of the department to which you are applying. Ask Human Resources for the correct spelling.

- Focus your letter on the employer's self-interest.

- Limit the letter to one page and use the same high-quality paper and printer you used for your resume. Address job qualifications listed in the vacancy announcement.

- Tailor each letter to a specific job and learn all you can about the employer.

- Write confidently without bragging or flattering. Be positive and direct.

- PROOFREAD! Have someone else look at the letter. No mistakes allowed.

- Don't forget to sign the letter. Omitting anything so simple is a sign of carelessness.

PART 7: PROOFREADING TIPS

The proofreading phase of the resume writing process is one of the most critical aspects of resume composition. You can have an outstanding resume that highlights your experience and credentials, but if it's covered with grammatical and formatting errors, this will be a big turnoff to the hiring officials, and it will generate weak or no reference from the HR Specialist. This section will explain ways to identify these mistakes and how to avoid them. Here are the basic things you can do to have a perfect resume, and remember you can use the same tips to proofread your cover letter:

- Read your resume slowly from beginning to end to identify inconsistencies, spelling errors, and other grammatical errors.

- Run it through your spell-check software to identify further mistakes you were initially unable to detect. But you should know that spell-check software isn't always 100% accurate. There are some grammatical errors it might not identify, so to be safe, try seeking a third/expert opinion before you submit.

- Since the resume comprises independent sections, you can read it section by section and compare it with format and arrangement, as has been mentioned in this book. And while you read, you should pay attention to sentence and paragraph length and makeup. The essence of this form of proofreading is that it forces you to pay attention to detail.

- To elaborate on the points given above, you should have a resume proofreading checklist. This gives you a list of what should be in your resume, the format it should be in, what should come before and after, the acceptable or preferred font size and style, and the language (this includes tone and style. The tone of your resume should be passive, while that of your cover letter should be active. The first person pronoun should not occur anywhere in your resume). Your proofreading checklist should identify spelling mistakes such as:

- When you use unrelated words (here you are not allowed to guess. Always have your dictionary with you).

- When you use wrong word forms (such as when there is a mix-up between "form" and "from," "there" and "their" spellcheck might not identify this sort of error).

- When you forget to use periods at the end of sentences. When typing your resume, ensure you click the space bar once instead of twice when a period ends a sentence and you begin a new sentence.

- When you are consistent in your style of punctuation and date format. If you have a need to use the quotation marks, ensure you maintain the kind you use. It is an error to mix the single and double quotation marks in a single document. And again, pay attention to quotation marks that end your sentences. If you have something like: Attended and excelled at the "Elizabeth Holden Writing Workshop." Take note to see how the period preceded the quotation mark. If you end the first bullet point with a period, maintain this throughout the book and vice versa.

- When you capitalize all proper nouns irrespective of where they appear in the sentence. Also, write your numbers in alphabets except for dates and those occurring in percentages. This goes to say that if you increased profit in your previous job, have it represented this way: "Increased profit by 55% by discovering and bridging the supply gap between warehouse and retail shops."

- When you check for word usage and establish that the appropriate words were used. This is because some words can be confusing. An example could be cited with words like affect (verb) effect (noun), personal and personnel.

- When you pay particular attention to your resume format: do not justify it, use a generally accepted font style like Times New Roman, unless the job announcement states otherwise, or overly use emphasizing features such as capitalization, bold/italics/underlines, and other such unnecessary features. Also, ensure you present your name and contact details in the same order. If you have Mary Lee McDermott on your resume, do not write McDermott Mary Lee on your cover letter. Choose a particular order and stick to it.

These are the essential resume proofreading tips you should adhere to if you don't want your resume to be trashed.

Top Secret Tip #19: Use the Resume Checklist as a guide when conducting your proofreading review. This way you are sure to cover every aspect of the resume during your proofreading check.

ADDITIONAL TIPS

To emphasize your skills, use action verb phrases (e.g., "organized a promotional campaign" or "developed and taught in-service courses"). Avoid first-person pronouns (e.g., "I," "me," "my") and phrases such as "duties included..." and "responsible for..." The current position should be written in the present tense; previous positions in the past tense of the verb. You should also pay attention to the following:

- Use popular, non-decorative typefaces.
- Use a font size of 10 to 12 points.
- Do not switch back and forth between typefaces and fonts.
- Use light-colored (white is best), standard size (8 1/2" x 11") paper.
- Avoid italic text, script, and underlined passages. Capitalized words and boldface are okay.

- Avoid graphics and shading. Don't compress spaces between letters.
- Avoid horizontal and vertical lines - they confuse the computer.
- Avoid staples and folds. If you must fold your resume, do not fold on a line of text.
- Your name should be the first readable item on each page.

JOSEPH MERCER

PART 8: FREQUENTLY ASKED QUESTIONS

In the business of consulting and writing resumes for clients, some questions that repeatedly arise. This section will address some of these questions and concerns, which you might be equally confused about. Some of the questions are:

1. ***Must I submit a resume to get an interview?***

    The answer to this question is the reason for this book, and, yes, you need a resume to get an interview. Recruiters and HR Specialists should know how you could be of benefit to the organization before they get you referred. The actual reason for submitting your Federal resume is not to get you into the interview.

I mean, your ultimate goal is to be interviewed for the position and eventually get hired. But the real purpose of a Federal resume is to establish your bona fides. In other words, this document serves as your proof of legitimacy and outlines your credentials and qualifications for the position being pursued.

2. *What should I include in my resume to get it noticed by the HR Specialist?*

To compete in today's market, you must know how to effectively present your skills, experience, knowledge, and background in a manner that will interest potential employers. Many well-qualified people are often not selected for job interviews because of poor resumes. A well-written resume will be noticed anywhere.

3. *Must my resume have an objective?*

This is not often required, but it is needful. Having an objective enables the HR Specialist to place your demands for the job and identify how you want to improve your career through your contributions to the growth of the company.

4. *What's the best format for a Federal resume?*

You should use the chronological order. This shows your experience and accomplishments from the most recent. It helps the HR Specialist establish your value concerning the job you are applying for.

5. *What's the best page length for my resume?*

There is usually no official number and limit, but generally, your Federal resume should be within two-five pages. If you already have an impressive career, it's best to keep it at four to five pages. All you have to do is to eliminate irrelevant work experience that might lengthen the pages. But for entry-level applicants, keep it at two pages. Foreground your academic achievements and include all necessary details within the two pages.

6. *In my job experience section, should I include unrelated jobs?*

If they will make your resume longer than five pages and if they will have no impact, exclude them. But if the achievements of these jobs will be a plus to your resume, by all means, include them. But make it as brief as possible.

7. *Should I include personal interests, such as hobbies and crafts?*

Personal interests are nice things to add in a resume; after all, they help the recruiter learn more about you. But the idea of a Federal resume is not to impress, but rather to express. If your personal interests do not express your abilities to do the job and if they will take up space, then you should not include them.

8. *Should my resume contain my GPA?*

If the application is entry-level, then you should flaunt your academic achievements.

9. *Are general headings such as education, experience consistently presented and emphasized by capitalizing, spacing, or bold-facing?*

They should be emphasized enough so that the HR Specialist can see them and understand that the points below elaborate them.

10. *Does the resume have an overall neat, readable appearance? Is it easy to scan? Is there sufficient but not excessive white space?*

The readability and neatness of your resume is a plus to you. I mean, who would want to waste time on an incomprehensible resume? Keeping it neat and simple does the trick.

11. *What are other tips do I need to succeed with my Federal Resume?*

Pay attention to all the tips in this book and also pay attention to the concerns raised in this FAQ section:

- Highlight special/unique skills.
- Highlight relevant experience.
- Proofread your resume.
- Use strong, action-oriented language.
- Remove items that are outdated (e.g., old technology, skill descriptions).
- Use past tense for work done in the past (e.g., organized) and present tense for work currently being done (e.g., organize).
- Use high-quality paper (white or cream).
- Use an 8 ½" x 11" envelope to avoid folding resumes.
- Fill gaps/time off with volunteer work.
- Use clear fonts (Arial, Times New Roman).
- Use a font size between 10-12 points.
- Be clear and concise.
- Have enough white space.
- Apostrophes indicate possession, contraction, or pluralized letters and numbers. It's easy to confuse it's (it is) with its (possessive of it). Generally, when nouns are possessive, the placement of the apostrophe indicates whether or not the noun is also plural. (Student's account indicates that something belongs to one of them, while students' indicate something belongs to more than one student.) You should know the difference.
- A verb must "agree with" its subject: Marie supervises, not Marie supervise. He does, but they do. These rules apply even when subjects and verbs are separated by other words and phrases. Pronouns must agree with the nouns to which they

refer: "A student must type their own resume" makes a lot of sense because grammar recognizes this possessive pronoun to be generic or genderless. Do not use his/her as possessive pronouns in such instances.

- Are any of your sentences overly long or overly short? Some short sentences can be combined with other sentences that have related ideas. Some, but not all, overly-long sentences are "run-on," which means that two independent clauses (a group of words containing a subject and predicate that can stand alone as a sentence) are fused together. You should prefer simple sentences.

12. *How far can I go on my work experience?*

The most important thing is to include your most relevant experience. When considering how far back to go with your work history, go as far back as you need to to make your experience applicable. In other words, make sure you highlight your accomplishments of previous jobs that are most recent and relevant to the position you are seeking.

13. *Should I submit references with my resume?*

It's best to save references for the interview stage unless they are specifically requested. Always get permission from your references before passing their information along to an employer. For more information about references, see A Guide to Outstanding Interviews.

14. *Can I include unpaid work experience (e.g., internships, co-op programs, volunteering)?*

Yes, you should if they are relevant to the position you are applying for and if they foreground your accomplishments.

15. *How do I handle gaps in my work experience?*

Dealing with gaps in work history can be tough for people, such as those who are re-entering the workforce after a long absence due to health issues, maternity leave, or incarceration. These and more like them cause gaps to appear in the experience. Other causes include work history consisting mostly of temporary or seasonal jobs. This often looks like "job-hopping." The solutions to these in your resume are:

- You could use a combination of functional resume format (only in this instance).
- List years instead of months and years.
- Don't emphasize dates (e.g., avoid bold text); de-emphasize with a smaller font.
- Include volunteer, consulting, or educational activities undertaken during employment gaps.
- Address employment gaps within your cover letter.
- Be prepared to provide honest answers about gaps in work history in an interview.

16. *What will I do if I just left college with little work experience or professional skills?*

You should apply within niches for entry-level, and when you do, foreground your academic accomplishments. Limited relevant experience can be an issue for those:

- Just entering the field.
- Changing careers.

The solutions include:

- Using a functional resume format.
- Considering your transferable skills.
- Incorporating the language of the job announcement.

- Connecting your skills to job requirements.
- Being open to learning.

17. *What if I am transferring from one department to another within the same agency?*

The truth is that various positions within a single company can be grouped together or listed separately. Indicate this in your cover letter and let your resume attest to it conspicuously.

18. *What if I want to apply with a degree I haven't been awarded yet?*

This is a common occurrence among college students, especially those in their senior year. The solutions to problems like this include:

- Listing incomplete education as "in progress" if you're still completing your studies and/or include an anticipated graduation date for your program.
- Listing what you have completed, regardless of whether you quit or are still "in progress." For instance, completed 30 credits towards BSc.
- Include high school or General Educational Development (GED) if you have no college/university credits.

19. *I'm new with minimal skills, what options do I have?*

Don't forget relevant training, seminars/workshops, and conferences. Like your physical appearance, your resume's appearance will make either a positive or negative impression on the employer. Using a standard template will result in a resume that looks like everyone else's. If you want your resume to grab the reader's attention, you'll need to invest a bit of time in creating it; allow several hours if this is your first resume or a major revision of an older one.

Make sure that your resume looks good and grabs the attention of your reader. Remember, no matter what design you choose for your resume, follow the Resume Tips in this guide, and review the resume.

CONCLUSION

This book has really exhausted the major challenges people face when they want to write a powerful Federal resume. Just like you were told at the beginning of this book, there wouldn't be any congratulations at the end because you will keep making reference to this book. So this is what this book has done: it has reminded you that there is a solution to writing Federal resumes, which can be found within the content of this book. Continue to reference it in the future, and you will have no worries.

JOSEPH MERCER

Appendix A: Top Secret Tips

- ✓ **Top Secret Tip #1:** The more you know about yourself and the position you are applying for, the more successful you will be at crushing the Federal resume creation process.

- ✓ **Top Secret Tip #2:** View the federal resume as a tool that you use in the initial phases of the job application process. Its purpose is to showcase the fact that you have the qualifications for the job you are seeking.

- ✓ **Top Secret Tip #3:** Make sure to read each Federal job announcement entirely and thoroughly. When you do, you will see a few job descriptions that fit your career avenue and your specific qualifications.

- ✓ **Top Secret Tip #4:** Make sure to thoroughly review the requirements in the vacancy announcement to include the minimum requirements and time-in-grade. Doing so will ensure that your resume has all the necessary information in it to meet these standards.

- ✓ **Top Secret Tip #5:** Make sure your resume has all the necessary information concerning your employment history listed. This includes past supervisor and salary information; not doing so could result in your resume not being processed for the position.

- ✓ **Top Secret Tip #6:** Always center your summary of qualifications statements around accomplishments that focus on the qualification requirements listed in the job announcement.

You want to tell the reader upfront that your resume will prove that you qualify for the position.

✓ **Top Secret Tip #7:** Use numbers, statistics, and quantifiable data when describing your achievements. This gives the HR Specialist a means to equate these to the position in which you are applying.

✓ **Top Secret Tip #8:** Don't forget (and this is a big one), your resume must cover all of the topics on the occupational assessment questionnaire. You can view this questionnaire by clicking the "view the Occupational Questionnaire" link under the "How to Apply" section of the job announcement.

✓ **Top Secret Tip #9:** Carefully consider which sections you include in your resume and how they are arranged. You want to make sure that the factors that qualify you for the position are highlighted prominently and upfront.

✓ **Top Secret Tip #10:** Take a break between the creation and review phases. You will come back to the project with a fresh perspective, and you are likely to see more issues.

✓ **Top Secret Tip #11:** It is important to be descriptive and thorough when telling about your skills and experience. Consider the HR Specialist and the hiring authority as being unfamiliar with tasks, systems, acronyms, terms, and other information about your current and past employment.

✓ **Top Secret Tip #12:** Use keywords and action words to describe your skills and experiences and always show how you used these attributes to add value to your organization.

✓ **Top Secret Tip #13:** Always request permission before offering someone as a reference. Also, provide them with a copy of your most current resume.

✓ **Top Secret Tip #14:** Address all qualification skills listed in a job announcement. Even if you are weak in a particular area, it is better to cover each qualifying factor than to have your resume dismissed for not meeting all the job qualification requirements.

✓ **Top Secret Tip #15:** When possible, end your experience "C.A.R." statements with quantitative and tangible results. Do not be modest, tell the hiring officials what you did that made an impact on the organizations in which you have worked.

✓ **Top Secret Tip #16:** Be sure to position your most qualifying skill factors in the first top quarter of the front page.

✓ **Top Secret Tip #17:** Never submit a Federal resume without a cover letter! The resume justifies that you qualify for the job with knowledge, skills, and abilities. The Cover letter shows that you fit the job in personality and attitude.

✓ **Top Secret Tip #18:** Always research the employer before creating your resume and cover letter. You can learn much about an organization's culture and mission from just doing a web search.

✓ **Top Secret Tip #19:** Use the Resume Checklist as a guide when conducting your proofreading review. This way, you are sure to cover every aspect of the resume during your proofreading check.

Appendix B: Resume Examples

Example 1

Example 1	**Logistics Management Specialist** GS-11-0346
Job Announcement	
Responsibilities	• Analyze statistics to determine trends in government and contractor-performed operations. • Coordinate with internal and external stakeholders to resolve readiness issues. • Develop primary contract documents, including Performance Work Statement (PWS), Procurement Package Information (PPI), and Independent Government Cost Estimates (IGCE). • Analyze contract cost, contractor performance, and scheduled milestones to verify accuracy, effectiveness, and compliance of operations to requirements. • Track readiness/maintenance status to ensure goals are met.
Qualifications Keywords highlighted in bold These are your application evaluation areas	**In order to qualify, you must meet the experience requirements below.** To qualify based on your experience, your resume must describe at least one year of experience. Specialized experience is defined as experience that is typically in or related to the work of the position to be filled, such as: • **Researching guidance, regulation, and/or policy** for applicability to supply/maintenance operations; • Supporting **Army Preposition Stocks (APS)** mission by identifying areas for improvement; and • Assisting with the development of **plans and work procedures** to accomplish the assigned mission. This definition of specialized experience is typical of work performed at the next lower grade/level position in the Federal service (GS-09). Creditable experience may include previous military experience, experience gained in the private sector, or in another government agency as long as it was at a level at least equivalent to the next lower band in the series. You will be evaluated based on your level of competency in the following areas: • Contracting/Procurement • Manages and Organizes Information • Organizational Performance Analysis • Technical Competence
Education	Education Substitution for Specialized Experience for GS-11: Successful completion of at least a Ph.D. or equivalent doctoral degree or three (3) full years of progressively higher-level graduate education leading to such a degree, or LL.M., if related, from an accredited college or university.

Example 1	**Logistics Management Specialist** GS-11-0346
Assessment Questionnaire	
Keyword Header	**Assessment Area**
Guidance, Regulation, and Policy Research	Experience in **researching guidance, regulation**, and/or **policy** for applicability to supply/maintenance operations.
Army Preposition Stocks (APS) Improvement	Experience in supporting **Army Preposition Stocks (APS)** mission by identifying areas for improvement.
Plans and Work Procedures Development	Experience assisting with the development of **plans and work procedures** to accomplish the assigned mission.
Reports/Briefings Preparation	**Prepare reports/briefings** to identify significant issues with assigned programs.
Info Papers	Write **info papers** in order to build program briefing charts for the assigned program.
Performance Analysis Measure	Develop assessment schedules for **performance analysis measures**.
Contract Execution Compliance	Ensure **contract** execution in **compliance** with requirements.
Communication	**Communicate** program requirements, constraints, and performance with all stakeholders.

Example 1: Resume (pg.1)

Andrew Wagner

77 Bellevue Dr., Painesville, OH 44077■ Home Phone 912-555-4929
■Email: drewagner45@gmail.com

LOGISTICS MANAGEMENT SPECIALIST
GS-0346-11
U.S. Training and Doctrine Command
Department of the Army

An accomplished Logistics Management Specialist with proven experience in providing outstanding results in support of Department of Defense logistical operations.

SUMMARY OF QUALIFICATIONS

- Over eleven years of demonstrated experience supporting contracting and procurement operations with extensive knowledge in the development of Performance of Work Statements (PWS), Statements of Work (SOW), and Independent Government Cost Estimates (IGCE)
- Over nine years of experience of independently managing and organizing information in support of logistics operations
- Seven years of experience performing organizational performance analysis on maintenance and logistics operations in support of Army mission and operations
- Over eleven years of demonstrated technical competence in the areas of logistical operations, contracting operations, analysis of contractor cost and performance, and tracking the readiness and status of equipment

SUMMARY OF EXPERIENCE

LOGISTICS MANAGEMENT SPECIALIST 02/2008 – PRESENT
Vego Logistics Group Inc. 40 hours per week
363 E. Lancaster Drive Salary: $52,000 USD per year
Great Neck, NY, USA Supervisor: Mark Veno 703-555-2455

Duty Summary. Serves as the Materiel Fielding Manager for the Material Fielding and Support Directorate responsible for the planning, and supervision of Army logistical operations. Responsibilities range from reporting, procurement, administration, and logistics.

Guidance, Regulation, and Policy Research. Demonstrates experience in researching guidance, regulation, and policy for supply operations. Researched applicable regulations pertaining to Army material fielding operations and developed desk references and process maps to assist units in the conducting of logistic operations. This effort made a positive impact on operations and productivity.

Accountability. Maintains accountability of a large inventory account used to support operational missions within the Army. Managed oversight of over $30 million in equipment ranging from combat vehicles to weapons systems. Maintained 100% accountability of all systems with zero losses in inventory.

Analysis and Reporting. Conducts analysis to identify issues with the logistical program and develop reports outlining recommendations for changes in plans, processes, policies, or procedures. Delivered an analysis-based report on the complex fielding process under the Total Package and Fielding (TPF) concept, resulting in a commendation for facilitating the equipment testing phase to sustainment operations ahead of schedule.

Project Management. Manages logistical projects to support supply and maintenance operations for the organization. Completed modification process project that included the validation and verification procedures of the MRAP 10/20 Reset Program and the Repair Parts Special Tools List. The modification process project was completed on time and without any issues.

Primary Contract Development. Prepares Performance Work Statements (PWS), Statement of Work (SOW), and Independent Government Estimates (ICGE). Negotiated contracts with potential vendors in support of the MRAP 10/20 Reset Program. Researched, summarized, and complied applicable data concerning obligations, expenses, and object line of accounting information, resulting in a negotiated savings for the Army of $20 million.

Accomplishments
- Developed and programmed budgets for combat weapon systems totaling over $4 billion during the budget cycle for FY 14-18
- Planned the physical relocation of the inventory to a new 40,000 sq. ft warehouse facility
- Oversaw operations and upkeep of 24 vehicles and 20 Mechanized Material Handling Systems valued at more than $26 million

ADDITIONAL EXPERIENCE NOT SHOWN FOR THIS EXAMPLE

JOSEPH MERCER

Example 1: Resume (pg.2)

SUMMARY OF EDUCATION

MASTER OF BUSINESS ADMINISTRATION: HUMAN RESOURCES   November 2010
Capella University, Minneapolis, Minnesota

BACHELOR OF SCIENCE: INTERNATIONAL BUSINESS MANAGEMENT   December 2008
Bluefield College, Bluefield, Virginia

ASSOCIATES OF SCIENCE: INTERNATIONAL BUSINESS MANAGEMENT   September 2006
Everest University, Tampa, Florida

PROFESSIONAL LICENSES/CERTIFICATIONS

- Army Acquisition Corps Membership (2012)
- TACOM Performance-Based Service Acquisition Training (2004)
- Level 3 Certified in Life Cycle Logistics (2007)
- Level 1 Certified in Program Management (2004)
- National Maintenance Logistics Modernization Program training (2009)
- National Maintenance Program (NMP) (2009)

AWARDS & RECOGNITIONS

- Performance Awards (2019, 2017, 2016, 2012, 2011, 2009, 2008)
- On spot awards (2014, 2012, 2011, 2010)
- Combined Force X Exercise Appreciation Letter (2020)
- Certificate of Appreciation (2019)

EXAMPLE 2

Example 1	**Logistics Management Specialist** GS-11-0346
Job Announcement	
Responsibilities	• Analyze statistics to determine trends in government and contractor-performed operations. • Coordinate with internal and external stakeholders to resolve readiness issues. • Develop primary contract documents, including Performance Work Statement (PWS), Statement of Work (SOW), and Independent Government Cost Estimates (IGCE). • Analyze contract cost, contractor performance, and scheduled milestones to verify accuracy, effectiveness, and compliance of operations to requirements. • Track readiness/maintenance status to ensure goals are met.
Qualifications **Keywords highlighted in bold** **These are your application evaluation areas**	In order to qualify, you must meet the experience requirements below. To qualify based on your experience, your resume must describe at least one year of experience. Specialized experience is defined as experience that is typically in or related to the work of the position to be filled, such as: • **Researching guidance, regulation, and/or policy** for applicability to supply/maintenance operations; • Assisting with the development of **plans and work procedures** to accomplish the assigned mission. This definition of specialized experience is typical of work performed at the next lower grade/level position in the Federal service (GS-09). Creditable experience may include previous military experience, experience gained in the private sector, or in another government agency as long as it was at a level at least equivalent to the next lower band in the series. You will be evaluated based on your level of competency in the following areas: • Contracting/Procurement • Manages and Organizes Information • Organizational Performance Analysis • Technical Competence
Education	Education Substitution for Specialized Experience for GS-11: Successful completion of at least a Ph.D. or equivalent doctoral degree or three (3) full years of progressively higher-level graduate education leading to such a degree, or LL.M., if related, from an accredited college or university.

Example 2	**Administrative Support Assistant** GS-07-0303	
Assessment Questionnaire		
Keyword Header	**Assessment Area**	
Budget Development	Experience in assisting in the development of annual, mid-year, and out-year budget.	
Accounts Management	Experience in establishing and maintaining accounts to ensure the availability of funds, and ensure that costs are charged to the appropriate accounts.	
Automation Skills	Experience in the use of word processing, databases, spreadsheets, graphics, electronic mail, and the internet/intranet to accomplish assignments.	
Scheduling and Calendars	Experience in maintaining electronic calendars for others to schedule appointments and meetings.	
Correspondence and Documentation	Experience in composing office memoranda, correspondence, and supporting documentation IAW rules, regulations, and policies.	

Example 2: Resume (pg.1)

Marion Barker

9117 SE. Buttonwood Street, Phoenixville, PA 19460 ■ Home Phone 475-555-7867
■Email: barker1977@outlook.com

ADMINISTRATIVE SUPPORT ASSISTANT
GS-0303-07
U.S. Army Element SHAPE
Department of the Army

Organized and professional Administrative Assistant with 15 years of experience in high-level executive support roles. Ability to create new systems and processes that improve efficiency and effectiveness of organizational operations. Instrumental in working with superior and departments in order to manage financial and accounting procedures.

SUMMARY OF SKILLS

- Account Management
- Administrative Support
- Operations Management
- Personnel
- Tracking Cash Flow
- Automation Skills
- Microsoft Word

- Scheduling and Calendars
- Document Preparation
- Data Analysis
- Annual Reports
- Budget Forecasting
- Time Keeping
- Correspondence Prep

- Bookkeeping
- Budget Development
- Database Entry
- Financial Systems
- Budget Concepts
- Microsoft Excel
- Microsoft PowerPoint

SUMMARY OF EXPERIENCE

ADMINISTRATIVE ASSISTANT
Vego Logistics Group Inc.
363 E. Lancaster Drive
Great Neck, NY, USA

02/2007 – PRESENT
40 hours per week
Salary: $32,000 USD per year
Supervisor: Davis Presley 703-555-2646

Duty Summary. Serves as the Administrative Assistant for Vego Logistics Group Inc., providing administrative support duties for 3 executives. Responsible for the preparation of sales reports, correspondence, and relevant documentation. Distributes information as directed and manages all incoming and outgoing mail for the shipping department.

Budget Development. Assists in the development of annual, mid-year, and out-year budget for the organization. Reviewed the budget submissions for completeness/accuracy and entered budget data into information management systems. Budget related projects were consistently free of error and adhered to relevant deadlines and timelines.

Accounts Management. Establishes and maintains accounts to ensure the availability of funds, and ensure that cost is charged to the appropriate accounts. Managed all accounts payable and receivable for the shipping department that grossed $1.7 million annually, without the presence of any delinquent or outstanding accounts.

Automation Skills. Utilize word processing, databases, spreadsheets, graphics, electronic mail, and the internet while conducting daily operations. Worked with the FoxPro database and other automation tools to manage and report on an inventory of over 10,000 accountable items. No accountable items were lost or misreported.

Scheduling and Calendars. Maintain and oversee electronic calendars for the shipping department for others to schedule appointments and meetings. Scheduled appointments and maintained calendars, arranged conference rooms, and facilities for executive-level meetings.

Correspondence and Documentation. Compose office memoranda, correspondence, and supporting documentation in accordance with organizational rules, regulations, and policies. Developed memorandums and correspondence quickly and error-free in support of 3 executives within the shipping division.

Accomplishments

- Maintained calendar and schedule for 3 executives, 250 employees, and 6 facilities
- Mentored new administrative assistant resulting in receiving the organization's Bronze Spirit Award
- Prepared itineraries, transportation arrangements, and expense reports valued at more than $150,000
- Developed and maintained accounts payable and receivable process that improved budget accuracy and efficiency

ADDITIONAL EXPERIENCE NOT SHOWN FOR THIS EXAMPLE

Example 2: Resume (pg.2)

SUMMARY OF EDUCATION

BACHELOR OF SCIENCE: BUSINESS ADMINISTRATION   June 2006
Bluefield University, Hampton, Virginia

ASSOCIATES OF SCIENCE: ACCOUNTING   December 2004
Regency School of Business, Atlanta, Georgia

PROFESSIONAL LICENSES/CERTIFICATIONS

- Certified Administrative Professional (2010)
- Certified Associate in Project Management (2016)
- Fundamental Payroll Certification (2007)
- Word 2010 Certification (2012)
- Microsoft Word 2013 Certification (2014)

AWARDS & RECOGNITIONS

- Performance Awards (2013, 2011, 2010, 2008)
- On spot awards (2018, 2015, 2012, 2010)
- Certificate of Appreciation (2016)
-

EXAMPLE 3

Example 3	**Maintenance Mechanic** WG-10-4749
Job Announcement	
Responsibilities	• You will determine the materials, tools, or equipment needed to perform and complete masonry assignments. • You will interpret instructions, sketches, blueprints, codes, or specifications to produce finished masonry work with precise fits, tight joints, and accurate dimensions. • You determine the grade, size, and precise type of lumber or wood substitute materials required to perform a carpentry job. • You will determine construction techniques for the fabrication, repair, or maintenance of wood or wood substitute structures.
Qualifications Qualifying Criteria	Although a specific length of time and experience is not required for most trade and labor occupations, you must show through experience and training that you possess the quality level of knowledge and skill necessary to perform the duties of the position at the level for which you are applying. Qualification requirements emphasis is on quality of experience, not necessarily the length of time. Your qualifications will be evaluated based on your level of knowledge, skills, abilities, and/or competencies in the job elements and screen out listed below. This job has a screen-out element that will be used to determine minimum eligibility for this job. Applicants who do not receive a minimum of two points on the screen-out element(s) will be found ineligible. The Screen-out Element for this position is the ability to perform the work of a Maintenance Mechanic WG-4749-10 as demonstrated by performing the following tasks: 1) Performs **construction of structures** such as doors, staircases, windows, interior and exterior trim, and associated building structures; 2) Performs **maintenance and repair** of exterior and interior surfaces and structures built of a variety of brick, block, and natural or artificial stone; and 3) **Plans and lays out projects.**
Education	N/A

(margin callouts: "These are your application evaluation areas")

Example 3	Maintenance Mechanic WG-10-4749		
Assessment Questionnaire			
Keyword Header	**Assessment Area**		
Material Estimates	Experience and/or training that demonstrates your ability to **estimate the type and quantity of material** (e.g., lumber, nails, mortises, dowels, glue) needed to complete carpentry projects.		
Structural Material Installation	Experience and/or training that demonstrates your ability to **install structural material** (e.g., brick, block, stone) in the construction or repair of partitions, walls, fireplaces, or walkways.		
Work Orders	Experience and/or training that demonstrates your ability to use materials (e.g., latches, hinges, nail moldings) specified in **work orders** for carpentry work.		
Determining Project Materials	Experience and/or training that demonstrates your ability to determine the grade, size, and type of lumber or special **materials** required for a **project**.		
Blueprints, Drawings, and Specifications	Experience and/or training that demonstrates your ability to read and interpret **blueprints, drawings, or specifications** to plan and complete assigned work.		

Example 3: Resume

Amy Bryan

866 Jones Street, Oakland Gardens, NY 11364 ■ Home Phone 542-555-1545
■Email: abryan1@yahoo.com

MAINTENANCE MECHANIC
WG-10-4749
Naval Facilities Engineering Command
Department of the Navy

Experienced Carpenter Assistant with a broad level of experience in the construction of structures and a strong understanding of all the basic fundamentals of carpentry. Skilled at managing a worksite and being responsible for carpentry equipment. Highly specialized in understanding complex architectural drawings and conducting maintenance and repairs on the exterior and interior surfaces.

SUMMARY OF SKILLS

- Ten years of experience determining materials, tools, and equipment required to perform masonry projects
- Ten years of experience interpreting construction sketches, blueprints, and specifications
- Ten years of experience determining the grade, size, and type of lumber and other materials used in carpentry
- Ten years of experience utilizing construction techniques for fabrication, repair, and maintenance of wood

SUMMARY OF EXPERIENCE

CARPENTER ASSISTANT   02/2010 – PRESENT
Vego Logistics Group Inc.   40 hours per week
363 E. Lancaster Drive   Salary: $35,000 USD per year
Great Neck, NY, USA   Supervisor: Jeffery Bierman 703-555-7265

Duty Summary. Serves as a Carpenter Assistant for Vego Logistics Group Inc., responsible for the installation and maintenance of footings, foundations, and interior and exterior trim of commercial projects. Additionally, responsible for determining the required materials for projects based on the provided plans and specifications.

Material Estimates Evaluates projects and deliver estimates on the type and quantity of material needed to complete required carpentry work. Reviewed blueprints to estimate the exact specification and requirements of a project to construct an addition to one of the company's warehouses. The project was delivered under budget, on time, and without any wasted materials.

Structural Material Installation. Installs structural material in the construction and repair of partitions, walls, fireplaces, and walkways. Competed for 14 construction and repair projects in 2018 ranging from brick and block walls to concrete walkways. Due to these efforts, all required construction and maintenance projects were handled internally to the company, thus eliminating the need for external contract support, which saved the organization money.

Work Orders. Use materials as specified in work orders to complete carpentry projects. Actioned approximately fifty work orders annually, each work order dictates the type of materials to be used to complete the work order project. No work orders have failed quality inspection upon completion.

Determining Project Materials. Determines the grade, size, and type of lumber or material required for each project. Read specifications on blueprints, building plans, or architectural sketches to prepare projects and determined dimensions and materials needed. Completed 10 construction projects in 1 year without any errors or waste in material due to selection.

Blueprints, Drawings, and Specifications. Read and interpret blueprints, drawings, and specifications to complete assigned work and projects. Reviewed blueprints to estimate exact specs and requirements of jobs and executed construction on more than 70 projects without error or excessive waste.

Accomplishments

- Conducted construction and maintenance operations for a complex comprised of sixteen facilities
- Mentored a new carpenter assistant resulting in an organizational leadership award
- Successfully interpreted blueprints and executed construction on a project valued at more than $1 million
- Completed over 14 construction and repair projects in one year; all under budget and with no delays

ADDITIONAL EXPERIENCE NOT SHOWN FOR THIS EXAMPLE

EXAMPLE 4

Example 4	Project Management Specialist (Facilities) GS-12-1601
Job Announcement	
Responsibilities	<ul><li>You will provide basic assistance to functional users regarding operation and maintenance and use approved troubleshooting techniques to test and analyze computer malfunctions</li><li>You will maintain a Local Area Network (LAN) receiving instructions and report and document LAN changes in status as they occur.</li><li>You will assist users with computer hardware/connectivity service requests.</li><li>You will maintain/interpret/write portions of operating equipment and user manuals and instructions.</li></ul>
Qualifications Keywords highlighted in bold Qualifying Criteria These are your application evaluation areas	**In order to qualify, you must meet the experience requirements described below.** **Specialized Experience:** One year of specialized experience which includes:<ul><li>Provide **technical advice on project scope, budget, and/or schedule.**</li><li>**Manage resource requirements** necessary for the execution of projects/programs.</li><li>Provide **resolutions for program/project deficiencies.**</li></ul>This definition of specialized experience is typical of work performed at the next lower grade/level position in the federal service (GS-11). You will be evaluated based on your level of competency in the following areas:<ul><li>Budget Administration</li><li>Program/Project Management</li><li>Technical Competence</li></ul>Time in Grade Requirement: Applicants who have held a General Schedule (GS) position within the last 52 weeks must have 52 weeks of Federal service at the next lower grade or equivalent (GS-11)
Education	Some federal jobs allow you to substitute your education for the required experience in order to qualify. For this job, you must meet the qualification requirement using experience alone--no substitution of education for experience is permitted.

Example 4	Project Management Specialist (Facilities) GS-12-1601
Assessment Questionnaire	
Keyword Header	**Assessment Area**
Technical Advice	Experience and/or training that demonstrates your ability to provide **technical advice** to project planners, managers, engineers, and/or architects to enhance future operations.
Requirement Management	Experience and/or training that demonstrates your ability to Identify, write, analyze, and/or **manage the requirements** of a project.
Recommendations	Experience and/or training that demonstrates your ability to anticipate potential problem areas and develop **recommendations** for solutions.
Analytical Methods	Experience and/or training that demonstrates your ability to utilize **analytical methods** to assess the status, effectiveness, and/or efficiency of facilities projects assigned.
Schedule Development	Experience and/or training that demonstrates your ability to read **develop** program/project **schedule** to meet deadlines, peak workloads, and priorities.

Example 4: Resume (pg.1)

Tonya Norris

7291 Sage Street, Sykesville, MD 21784 ■ Home Phone 221-555-6815
■Email: tonya-norris@gmail.com.com ■ Veteran's Preference: 30 Points

PROJECT MANAGEMENT SPECIALIST (FACILITIES)
GS-1601-12
U.S. Army Corps of Engineers
Department of the Army

Process-driven Project Management professional with 15+ years of proven experience directing multiple projects to successful completion through effective management and team collaboration. In-depth understanding of project management standards, project engineering, and controls. Motivated leader and communicator who builds cohesion, trust, and project management engagement across all levels of stakeholders.

SUMMARY OF SKILLS

• Stakeholder Engagement	• Complex Decision Making	• Contract Management
• Project Management	• Database Management	• Risk Analysis
• Empowerment Leadership	• Needs Assessment	• Planning & Scheduling
• Earned Value Analysis	• Problem Solving	• Workflow Documentation

SUMMARY OF EXPERIENCE

FACILITIES PROJECT MANAGER   02/2015 – PRESENT
Vego Logistics Group Inc.   40 hours per week
363 E. Lancaster Drive   Salary: $67,000 USD per year
Great Neck, NY, USA   Supervisor: Thomas Lasch 703-555-1061

Duty Summary. Serves as the Facilities Project Manager for Vego Logistics Group Inc., providing construction project management, customer service, and project development. Responsible for coordination with sub-contractors, material suppliers, and vendors to ensure that quality, budget, and schedule requirements are achieved.

Scheduling and Budget Commitments. Ensures adherence to schedule and budget commitments through regular analysis, reporting, and oversight. Implemented an improved project database capable of continually monitoring both scheduled operations and budgetary considerations. The new system allows the organization to analyze project needs, including project plans, budgets, and schedules.

Requirement Management. Identifies, writes, analyzes, and manages requirements for projects. Provides detailed reports, leads project reviews, spearheads issue resolution discussions, leads process development, and the gathering and integrating of requirements from cross-functional stakeholders and external vendors. Responsible for project requirements on a $30 million critical infrastructure construction project. All requirements were identified and managed to completion.

Recommendations. Anticipate potential problem areas and develop recommendations for solutions. Implemented a SharePoint program that provided a detailed list of all program action items, risk, opportunity, and issues. The database was set-up to not only assign tasks but also to document issue ownership and mitigation plans. This effort resulted in a 50% reduction in the time required to identify and resolve project issues.

Analytical Methods. Utilize analytical methods to assess the status, effectiveness, and efficiency of facilities projects. Consolidated and analyzed project information to present weekly and monthly performance reporting packages; communicated plan changes and recovery plans to management and customers. These analytics were then used to negotiate settlements with contractors and vendors.

Schedule Development. Read and develop project schedules to meet deadlines, peak workloads, and priorities. Analyzed project requirements, including project plans and delivery schedules, established project management strategies, and recommended the appropriate level of planning, scheduling, and control.

Accomplishments

- Managed 174 successful construction projects in five years with an average budget of $1.5 million
- Implemented numerous tools for site survey, budgeting, bidding, and project tracking
- Reduced construction cost and timelines for over 100 construction projects via cost-saving methods

ADDITIONAL EXPERIENCE NOT SHOWN FOR THIS EXAMPLE

Example 4: Resume (pg.2)

SUMMARY OF EDUCATION

MASTER OF SCIENCE: BUSINESS ADMINISTRATION   January 2012
University of California, Santa Barbara, California

BACHELOR OF SCIENCE: BUSINESS ADMINISTRATION   June 2009
Stanford University, Stanford, California

PROFESSIONAL LICENSES/CERTIFICATIONS

- Project Management Professional (PMP) (2014)
- CompTIA Project+ (2010)
- Master Project Manager (MPM) (2016)

AWARDS & RECOGNITIONS

- Performance Awards (2015, 2011, 2010, 2008)
- On spot awards (2018, 2015, 2012, 2010)
- Certificate of Appreciation (2017)

EXAMPLE 5

Example 5	**IT SPECIALIST (SYSADMIN)** GS-09-2210
Job Announcement	
Responsibilities	• You will provide basic assistance to functional users regarding operation and maintenance and use approved troubleshooting techniques to test and analyze computer malfunctions • You will maintain a Local Area Network (LAN) receiving instructions and report and document LAN changes in status as they occur. • You will assist users with computer hardware/connectivity service requests. • You will maintain/interpret/write portions of operating equipment and user manuals and instructions. • You will assist in the management of information technology projects to include the planning, executing, and closing of the project.
Qualifications *Keywords highlighted in bold* *These are your application evaluation areas*	In order to qualify, you must meet the experience requirements below. Specialized Experience: One year of specialized experience which includes: • **Planning, developing and carrying out the daily operations of a Local Area Network** (LAN) • **Maintenance and accountability** of computer hardware and software and training personnel on the best use of available software You will be evaluated based on your level of competency in the following: • Attention to Detail • Project Management • Networking • Emerging Technologies
Education *Educational Qualifying Criteria*	The following education can be substituted for experience: Successfully completed a master's or equivalent graduate degree from an accredited or pre-accredited institution in computer science, engineering, information science, information systems management, mathematics, operations research, statistics, or technology management; or, graduate education that provided a minimum of 24 semester hours in one or more of the fields identified above and required the development or adaptation of applications, systems or networks. OR Successfully completed 2 full years (36 hours) of progressively higher graduate level education leading to a master's degree or equivalent graduate degree from an accredited or pre-accredited institution in computer science, engineering, information science, information systems management, mathematics, operations research, statistics, or technology management; or, graduate education that provided a minimum of 24 semester hours in one or more of the fields identified above and required the development or adaptation of applications, systems or networks.

Example 5	IT SPECIALIST (SYSADMIN) GS-09-2210		
Assessment Questionnaire			
Keyword Header	**Assessment Area**		
Attention to Detail	Demonstrated competence in being thorough when performing work and conscientious about **attending to detail**.		
Project Management	Demonstrated competence in the **management** of information technology projects to include the planning, executing, and closing of the **project**.		
Networking	Demonstrated competence in the ability to maintain a **Local Area Network** (LAN) receiving instructions and report and document LAN changes in status as they occur.		
Troubleshooting	Demonstrated competence in the ability to research and stay current on emerging technologies.		

Example 5: Cover Letter

Earnest Duncan

220 W. Leeton Ridge Dr., Hazleton, PA 18201 ■ Home Phone 983-555-6107
■Email: earnestduncan11@gmail.com

IT SPECIALIST (SYSADMIN)
GS-09-2210
U.S. Marine Corps
Department of the Navy

February 28, 2020

Dear Staffing Representative:

Please accept my application for the position of IT Specialist with the U.S. Marine Corps. The U.S. Marine Corps is a time-honored organization since 1775 with a reputation for excellence and comradery. I believe that my commitment to excellence and extensive knowledge of information technology makes me an ideal candidate for this position with your organization.

As a recent graduate of Pennsylvania State University, I have developed an extensive background in information technology. As an information system management major, I held multiple internships, including an IT coordinator Intern at Vego Logistics Group Inc. I also served as president of the technology club at school. We successfully developed and pitched Science, Technology, Engineer, and Math (STEM) training programs for local elementary schools.

Your job announcement indicated that you are looking for someone with strong project management skills and attention to detail. Throughout my six years of college, I worked part-time as a customer support representative for a bottled water distributor. This job required great attention to detail and the ability to work on multiple projects at once.

These strengths, combined with a deep and varied academic, internship, and employment experience, have prepared me for this position.

Thank you in advance for your time and review of my credentials.

Sincerely

Earnest Duncan

Example 5: Resume

Earnest Duncan
220 W. Leeton Ridge Dr., Hazleton, PA 18201 ■ Home Phone 983-555-6107
■Email: earnestduncan11@gmail.com

IT SPECIALIST (SYSADMIN)
GS-09-2210
U.S. Marine Corps
Department of the Navy

SUMMARY OF EDUCATION

MASTER OF SCIENCE: INFORMATION SYSTEMS MANAGEMENT (32 semester hours)	2019
Pennsylvania State University (accredited)	Graduated (cum laude)
University Park, PA, USA	3.9 GPA

Degree Summary. The Master's in information technology degree program teaches students how to use the latest technology in the information technology industry to solve problems within the business, the government, and other types of organizations. It introduces the student to advanced management skills making them effective communicators and decision-makers. This course also teaches the student to become a leader and innovator in several specific information technology areas.

Attention to Detail. Demonstrated competency in being thorough when performing work and conscientious about attending to detail. Graduated cum laude with a 3.9 GPA in a program based on detail-oriented courses such as software design, data science, computer programming, and software development.

Project Management. Trained in the management of information technology projects to include the planning, executing, and closing of the project. Successfully completed the Project Management Fundamentals course, which requires learners to develop and demonstrate their understanding of project management concepts as defined by the Project Management Institute's (PMI) A Guide to the Project Management Body of Knowledge (PMBOK© Guide).

Networking. Trained in the ability to maintain a Local Area Network (LAN) receiving instructions and report and document LAN changes in status as they occur. Successfully completed Security and Enterprise Networks course, requiring learners to examine the concepts of enterprise network design, core network infrastructure hardware, configuration, and architecture of computing networks. Learners also acquire training and knowledge on network security, firewalls, VPNs, and network protocols.

Emerging Technologies. Trained in the ability to research and stay abreast of emerging information technologies. Successfully completed the Emerging Technologies Course, which taught new and disruptive technologies that are poised to have a significant impact on society and organizations. In this course, learners explore strategies for researching and identifying emerging technologies in order to determine their value to organizational models.

ADDITIONAL EXPERIENCE NOT SHOWN FOR THIS EXAMPLE

APPENDIX C: RESUME DEVELOPMENT WORKSHEETS

RESUME DEVELOPMENT PROCESS

COLLECT	**Collection Checklist**
	☐ Keywords from job announcement
	☐ Old resumes (if applicable)
	☐ Employment information
	☐ College Transcripts
	☐ Contact information for current and past supervisors
	☐ Addresses for current and past employers
	☐ Addresses for volunteer and civic organization
	☐ Copies of awards and recognitions (if applicable)

PREPARE	Experience Worksheet	Accomplishments Worksheet	Education Worksheet
	• Enter experience info for each position	• Enter professional & personal/social/civic accomplishments	• Enter info for each advanced education
	• Provide short duty description for positions	• Provide relevant skills associated with each accomplishment	• Provide short description of relevant studies
	• List organizational impacts		• List awards & honors
	• Enter C.A.R statements		• Provide overall GPA

CREATE	Format Checklist	Resume Creation
	☐ Select resume format	• Apply selected format from Format Checklist
	☐ Define resume sections	• Import header from Format Checklist
	☐ Select font & points size	• Import work history from Experience Worksheet
	☐ Determine overall resume look/design	• Import accomplishments from Accomplishments Worksheet
	☐ Develop Resume Header	• Import education history from Education Worksheet
		• Import awards and recognitions from Collection Checklist

REVIEW	Resume Checklist	Proofreading	Trusted Reviewer
	• Check overall format	☐ Identify misspelled words	• Evaluate attractiveness
	• Check Heading section	☐ Wrong word forms	• Check for grammar mistakes
	• Check Education section	☐ Format inconsistencies	• Evaluates style and grammar
	• Check Experience section	☐ Grammar mistakes	• Examines the overall resume look/design
	• Check Honors & Awards section	☐ No Personal pronouns	
		☐ No weak action verbs	

Download copy of worksheet at www.career-motivation.com

EXPERIENCE WORKSHEET

Company Name				
City			State	
State Date		End Date		

Position Title	
Duty Description	

List below where you made an impact on this organization	
1	
2	
3	
4	

What actions did you take to achieve the impacts listed above? (write them in CAR story format): Challenge / Action / Result. Include tangible (quantitative and qualitative) descriptions for these impacts.
CAR #1
Challenge Statement
Action Statement
Result Statement
CAR #2
Challenge Statement
Action Statement
Result Statement
CAR #3
Challenge Statement
Action Statement
Result Statement
CAR #4
Challenge Statement
Action Statement
Result Statement

Download copy of worksheet at www.career-motivation.com

ACCOMPLISHMENT WORKSHEET

Professional:

Accomplishment	Skills

Personal / Social / Civic:

Accomplishment	Skills

Download copy of worksheet at www.career-motivation.com

EDUCATION WORKSHEET

College/University Name			
City		State	
Completion Date			

Major	
Course Description	

List below where you made an impact on this organization	
1	
2	
3	
4	

What academic experience did you receive that is relevant to the position in which you are applying.
Statement #1
Statement #2
Statement #3
Statement #4

Download copy of worksheet at www.career-motivation.com

RESUME CHECKLIST

Overview	Yes	No
Is the resume the appropriate length for the experience level and grade (2-5 pages)?		
Is the layout of the resume inviting, with consistent formatting, fonts, and font sizes?		
All information is presented in a logical and well organized manner.		
Are all the sections of the resume clearly label?		
All margins are consistent and even on all sides.		

Heading	Yes	No
Does heading include your name, address, email address, and phone number?		
Are you using your formal name without abbreviations?		
Is you email address professional?		

Education	Yes	No
Does the education section outline your school name and address?		
Is the major and minor indicated for all degree plans?		
Does the section highlight training, certifications and licenses relevant to the position?		
Does the section list the institution with the city and state, and your graduation date?		
Education information includes academic honors received.		

Experience	Yes	No
Is experience listed in reverse chronological order (present or newest job first)?		
Does each position include a solid listing of accomplishments?		
Does the section present experience using the CAR format?		
Does each description statement begin with a strong action verb?		
Does the experience being highlighted seem relevant to the requirements of the position?		
Are specific keywords from the job announcement and other sources being used?		
Is required information (company address, supervisor's name, etc.) included?		

Honors and Awards	Yes	No
Only scholarships that are based on merit, not financial need are included.		
Descriptions are included with each award to highlight the nature of the accomplishment.		
Military awards are listed in chronological order with a brief description on the award.		

Proofreading	Yes	No
Spell check is used to identify commonly misspelled words.		
A manual proofreading was conducted to check for wrong word forms ("form" and "from").		
Read resume section by section and compare format and arrangement of each section.		
Has a second person read over your resume paying attention to style an grammar?		
Have you avoided the use of personal pronouns (I, me, and my)?		
The resume is error-free (no spelling errors, typos, grammar mistakes, etc.).		
The formatting is consistent (bold, underlining, and fonts).		

Download copy of worksheet at www.career-motivation.com

ACTION VERB LIST

Accomplishments	achieved expanded improved pioneered reduced resolved	 restored spearheaded transformed operationalized	Management	administered analyzed assigned attained oversaw consolidated	improved delegated organized developed directed recommended
Communication	wrote collaborated influenced negotiated promoted addressed	arbitrated arranged authored drafted directed convinced	Technical	assembled built calculated computed designed devised	engineered fabricated maintained operated programmed upgraded
Teaching	advised clarified coached instructed coordinated developed	enabled encouraged explained facilitated informed coached	Financial	administered allocated analyzed appraised audited balanced	forecasted managed marketed planned projected researched
Creative	acted fashioned created customized developed directed	initiated instituted integrated introduced invented originated	Helping	assessed assisted clarified coached counseled demonstrated	familiarized guided motivated referred rehabilitated represented
Clerical	approved arranged catalogued classified collected compiled	dispatched executed generated implemented inspected monitored	Detail Oriented	operated organized prepared processed purchased recorded	retrieved screened specified systematized tabulated validated
Data	Calculated Compared Composed Computed Complied Conducted	Planned Recorded Reported Researched Synthesized Theorized	People	Advised Assessed Coordinated Consulted Counseled Entertained	Instructed Interviewed Led Managed Motivated Negotiated

Avoid weak verbs such as: assisted, aided, helped, handled, participated in, responsible for, used, worked with, oversaw, etc. Instead, select verbs that create a picture of you in action. Follow the verb with the success or result of that action.

Download copy of worksheet at www.career-motivation.com

Made in the USA
Middletown, DE
19 June 2021

42779551R00084